The NEWSLETTER HANDBOOK

How to Write and Publish Newsletters

Wesley Dorsheimer

HIPPOCRENE BOOKS
New York

ACKNOWLEDGMENTS

Special thanks to the publishers, editors, and others I spoke with at the more than 100 newsletters discussed in the book. In particular, I thank these individuals for all their help — from interviews to sign-off. I especially thank my wife, Patricia, for assistance in proofreading and for being understanding on the countless occasions when I disappeared to my word processor.

Thanks also to Ace Graphics Inc. (Tenafly, NJ) for providing information on the start-up example in Chapter Six.

For information, address:
HIPPOCRENE BOOKS, INC.
171 Madison Avenue
New York, NY 10016

Library of Congress Cataloging-in-Publication Data
Dorsheimer, Wesley.
The newsletter handbook : how to write and publish newsletters / Wesley Dorsheimer.
p. m.
ISBN 0-7818-0124-9
1. Newsletters—Publishing. I. Title.
Z286.N46D67 1993 93-17443
070.1'75—dc20 CIP

Printed in the United States of America

CONTENTS

TABLES

FIGURES

CHAPTER ONE

Summary

What the Book's All About

1.1 Overview

The *Newsletter Handbook* is a guide to writing and publishing newsletters. It describes 90 how-to steps for producing successful newsletters. For example, the book presents practical steps on getting ready to publish, building a profitable newsletter venture, and establishing an ongoing relationship with your readers. Such key matters as how to register a copyright, how often to publish, and whether or not to include advertising are also discussed. Among the 90 how-to steps are the specifics of starting up a 4-page newsletter, how to improve newsletter uniformity with a style guide, and when to use word processing and desktop publishing.

1.2 Q&A Highlights

The book breathes life and practicality into all 90 steps by highlighting specific examples of more than 100 of today's newsletters. Among the examples cited are current newsletters in the fields of computers, accounting, library science, investments, banking, landscaping, food protection, health, and dentistry. Also discussed are newsletters in the areas of instrumentation, business, printing, electronics, graphics, government waste, museums, science, finance, and many others.

In a sense, the book is woven from two threads. One is a list of steps (as described in the book) for producing or upgrading a newsletter; the other is a random selection of over 100 of today's newsletters. The newsletter examples illustrate the various steps in launching a newsletter or upgrading an existing one. Here in CHAPTER ONE are some of the book's highlights, presented in Q&A form:

Q. What's the prime essential for people planning to launch or upgrade a newsletter?

A. First, suggests the book, ask yourself some key questions, such as:

- What is the main information your readers are seeking?
- Who are the potential readers who will find your newsletter of value?
- Will your potential readers have to pay for the newsletter out of their own pockets, or do they work for companies who will pay for it?

❑ ❑ ❑

Q. What do readers consider most important in a newsletter?

A. Readers want information they can use immediately.

❑ ❑ ❑

Q. How can money be saved in printing a newsletter?
A. One of the biggest costs results from lack of thorough proofreading. Remember, though, you only pay the typesetter for writer's alterations, not for typesetting errors.

❑ ❑ ❑

Q. How many different newsletters are being published today?
A. One directory, "Newsletters in Print," lists more than 10,000 major newsletters, bulletins, and other publications — over 5,000 of which sell for subscriptions ranging from several dollars to more than $500 per year. Another directory, the "Oxbridge Directory of Newsletters: 1991," lists 21,000 newsletters in its ninth edition.

But the number of newsletters listed by directories is only a drop in the bucket. Newsletters listed in directories represent only a fraction of the total number presently being published. What's the explanation? Directories often exclude one-time-only newsletters, local publications, and newsletters not generally available to the public. Some directories also exclude house organs and internal corporate newsletters. When all types of newsletters are considered, though, the total may be as high as 200,000 or more published per year.

❑ ❑ ❑

Unfortunately, there's no consensus as to precisely what consititutes a newsletter. For our purposes, the working definition for "newsletter" used in this publication is:

A publication issued on a timely basis in accordance

with a set schedule (or published intermittently), and called a newsletter by its publisher. A newsletter may be of any length, and may (or may not) carry space advertising. When feature articles are included, these may (or may not) contain references or a bibliography.

❑ ❑ ❑

Q. In what ways do today's newsletters differ from those of the past?

A. In general, today's newsletters are turned around more quickly, display more savvy in presenting complex subjects, exhibit greater candor in discussing the realities of the times, and enjoy larger circulations. In all, five basic types of newsletters are presently being published:

(1) The subscription newsletter is the newsletter in which people caught up with the entrepreneurial spirit are most interested. Annual subscriptions to this type of newsletter can run as high as $800 or more. Subscribers consider the information so valuable that they (or their companies) are willing to pay top dollar for a subscription. Many subscription newsletters, such as "The Kiplinger Washington Letter" or "Control Industry Inside Report," are written in abbreviated form to meet the requirements of today's busy executives. Today's readers want instantaneous, concise answers to such questions as: Who's involved? What's at stake? and What's ahead?

(2) The special-interest group (SIG) newsletter contains information for people having a common interest, such as a concern for computer-generated graphics ("Computer Graphics") or a love of animals ("The Latham Letter"). "LAMALUG: The Apple COREspon-

dent," for example, contains information about Apple products, and fields such questions as, Can I take a tax deduction for the Mac that I use in my work?

When a newsletter is successful, its publisher is often tempted to issue others. This accounts (at least in part) for the many multiple-newsletter publishers, such as the Association for Computing Machinery, Inc. (ACM). A membership association for computing and information processing, ACM has more than 30 special-interest groups, each of which publishes its own newsletter dealing with a particular subject. ACM's special-interest group, SIGGRAPH, for example, publishes "Computer Graphics."

(3) A third type of newsletter is the organization newsletter. It's typically issued by a nonprofit organization or branch of government for its members and employees. Belonging to the organization entitles members to receive copies of the newsletter.

It's important, explains the book, that organization newsletters keep in close touch with members, providing them with a balanced perspective on news of the organization. Thus, the Arthritis Foundation, New Jersey Chapter publishes "The Newsletter," which is issued to 40,000 members, three times a year. In April 1991, "The Newsletter" was officially recognized for achieving a balanced mixture of news; the publication was awarded second place in the 4th Annual Newsletter Contest for nonprofit organizations. In this contest — which was sponsored by Pro Bono, Inc., volunteers in public relations (Madison, NJ) — 41 newsletters were entered from throughout New Jersey.

(4) Another type of newsletter is the corporate newsletter, with both inside and outside versions. The

inside corporate newsletter, also known as a house organ or internal newsletter, is breaking with tradition these days. A growing number of corporate communications specialists believe that company publications should reflect the new realities of life in the workplace. By being more candid, they believe newsletters can communicate with employees more effectively. Similarly, letters to the editor that are critical of the corporation are being printed today in the company newsletter — when they wouldn't previously have passed the first level of management approval.

The outside corporate newsletter, although published primarily for external distribution, is usually distributed internally as well. Thus, "News notes," an outside corporate newsletter, presenting information on the company's latest instrumentation, is mailed to users at no charge, and is also distributed internally.

(5) Among a variety of miscellaneous newsletters described are the promotional newsletter, the franchise newsletter, and newsletters published for the well-being of the public. Promotional newsletters are not always what they seem; designed to look as though they contain valuable information, they are, in fact, sales pitches. Franchise, or syndicated, newsletters provide publishers with the benefits of communicating with their clients, while holding down publication costs. A company can purchase a supply of these preprinted franchise publications, imprint its name and logo, add its own message (when desirable), and distribute finished newsletters.

❑ ❑ ❑

Not all newsletters fit neatly into one or another of

these five main classifications, however, explains the book. Note the following uses of newsletters:

- A publisher may issue two newsletters dealing with the same subject matter but targeted for different audiences. Thus, "Dynamic Supervision," a newsletter published by the Bureau of Business Practice (BBP), provides tips on supervisory methods in a plant setting. At the same time, "Dynamic Supervision — Office and Staff Edition," another BBP newsletter, deals with the same subject, but in an office setting.
- Sometimes a publisher produces two entirely different types of publications dealing with the same subject — such as a newsletter and a journal. Pierian Press, for example, publishes "Library Hi Tech News," a 32-page newsletter, and, at the same time, "Library Hi Tech," a journal that's three times as long as the newsletter.
- Some newsletters are offered to subscribers as part of a larger package. The Bureau of National Affairs, Inc., (BNA), for example, publishes "Payroll Administration Guide Newsletter," a biweekly. Included with each annual subscription to this newsletter is BNA's "Payroll Administration Guide." This guide consists of a five-binder notification and reference package for payroll managers.
- In addition, newsletter readers have a choice of in-print newsletters, on-line newsletters, and newsletters that are available both in print and on line. Readers can also obtain faxed newsletters, newsletters on diskette, and audio cassettes for the blind.

❑ ❑ ❑

Q. How can newsletter uniformity be improved? What's the best way to standardize abbreviations, acronyms, and other parameters of the printed page?

A. Try using a stylebook. Communicators point out that they're used by almost a quarter of all newsletters. "Apple Library Users Group (ALUG) Newsletter," for example, is published for users of Apple computers in libraries and information centers. "ALUG" uses a style guide routinely for such purposes as proper placement of the dash and how to handle illustrations. The style guide is loaded on a DTP system comprised of a Macintosh II, PageMaker 4.0, and a LaserWriter MTX.

Other users of style guides include the Library of Michigan (style guides are set electronically on file servers for each of its 10 newsletters) and Warren Publishing, Inc. (a style guide is used for such things as setting standards for acronyms and abbreviations in its 12 newsletters).

❑ ❑ ❑

Q. In addition to use of a style manual, is there any other way to achieve better newsletter uniformity?

A. Try issuing writer's guidelines. Pinnacle Publishing, Inc., for example, produces seven subscription newsletters dealing with database programs of various software manufacturers. In its newsletters, Pinnacle makes wide use of case studies in which freelance authors tell how they use database programs. Pinnacle's newsletters are usually 16 to 24 pages in length; contributed articles run eight or more pages in length. To achieve some measure of uniformity among articles, Pinnacle issues writer's guidelines to its freelance authors.

❑ ❑ ❑

Q. Are you considering the installation of a word processor?
A. You would be in good company. Word processors such as WordPerfect, WordStar, Lotus Manuscript, and Express Publisher offer quality that comes very close to DTP and typesetting.

❑ ❑ ❑

Q. Are you thinking of installing DTP?
A. Newsletter publishing is probably the one area of publishing where DTP is best suited:

- Newsletters are often 8 1/2 by 11 inches — the size that IBM PCs and Macintosh computers are best at creating.
- Newsletters usually have small staffs — often only one or two people. Hence, they can readily change methods to make the most effective use of DTP.
- Typeset copy takes up less space than typescript. Thus, DTP provides more information per page and lower printing and mailing costs.
- DTP allows typography to be used creatively.
- Even a partial DTP system can be used to publish a newsletter.

❑ ❑ ❑

DTP can be useful regardless of the size of the task it's asked to handle. At the Library of Michigan, for example, almost 900 publications are produced electronically — including five regularly scheduled newsletters and others issued sporadically. A computer network makes it possible to produce material for publications on any of about 50 Macintosh computers and 15 laser printers.

Other publishers using DTP include the Association for Computing Machinery, Inc., (Many of its newsletters are produced using desktop publishing) and Warren Publishing, Inc., who routinely uses DTP to publish nine of its 12 newsletters.

DTP can also be used effectively by individuals; even one person using DTP can easily perform all the tasks involved.

Q. How well do newsletters do in getting out information quickly?

A. In fact, this is one area where newsletters excel. Take "Library Hotline," for instance, a newsletter published by the Bowker Magazine Group of Cahner's Publishing Company. "Library Hotline" generally reaches its readers less than six days after submission of copy, according to its editor, Susan DiMattia.

❑ ❑ ❑

Q. How do newsletters receive their titles and subtitles?

A. In deciding on a newsletter title, it's advantageous that it describe either the newsletter's subject matter or its target audience — or both. It's also recommended that the title be clever — if possible. For example, the newsletter "Moneysworth" prospered and eventually became a magazine when its circulation grew to more than half a million subscribers. Its catchy title probably helped boost sales.

Other titles that give an indication of content are "mixin'" (American Bartender's Association), "The Migrant" (Michigan Audubon Society), and "New Waves" (Texas Water Resources Institute-Texas A&M University). A newsletter's title, however, is not always an indication of its contents.

Subtitles are often used to explain puzzling titles. The newsletter ".dbf," for example, carries the subtitle: "The authoritative dBase monthly."

❑ ❑ ❑

Q. Are Q&A columns often published in newsletters?

A. Yes. Columns go well in newsletters. Take the two following examples: The "Printing Association of Florida Newsletter" frequently contains the column, "Q&A: Dear Marion," written by Marion Clark, president of Unemployment Services, Inc., a private company which helps Florida employers fight improper unemployment claims and reduce unemployment taxes. The column discusses such matters as the impact of legislation on industry.

In another area, consider the newsletter "Science Watch," published by ISI Institute for Scientific Information (Philadelphia, PA): The newsletter, which is published ten times a year, contains a Q&A column in each issue. Over a third of the newsletter's November 1990 issue, for example, is devoted to a Q&A article about the new trans-Pacific fiber-optic communications line scheduled to be laid by 1996.

❑ ❑ ❑

Q. What are the problems of using case histories in newsletters?
A. Always obtain the right person's ok to start, and, if sign-off is necessary, refrain from giving out copies of your write-up until final approval has been obtained.

❑ ❑ ❑

Q. Is there any particular type of software that's especially effective for creating complex newsletters?

A. Windows word processors, an increasingly popular category of software, are very useful for designing multi-column layouts and complicated newsletters.

❑ ❑ ❑

Q. Is there any reason for obtaining a sign-off when it isn't actually required?
A. There are several reasons for obtaining a sign-off, other than obtaining approval; for one, it will help you to know whether your facts are correct.

❑ ❑ ❑

Q. What input sources are used most frequently when publishing a newsletter?
A. Useful information sources are as varied as letters to the editor and on-line databases. On the first score, a typical 42-page issue of "The Portable Paper," for example, contains as many as 10 letters to the editor. And probably even more newsletters use database input. Among the newsletters using database input is "Dun's Dataline," published by Dun's Marketing Services, a Company of the Dun & Bradstreet Corporation. "Dun's Dataline" is published for its customers worldwide, providing in-

formation about Dun & Bradstreet's databases on Dialog. (Dialog has over 380 databases.)

❑ ❑ ❑

Q. Is information available on newsletter start-up?
A. This book presents specific steps for starting up a 4-page newsletter ... from setting objectives and establishing a basic design ... to using reply cards and order forms. Using sophisticated computer programs, you can now reproduce many sizes and styles of type — and print out newsletters that are almost as high in quality as those printed with typographical equipment. Typically, computer, software, and laser printer can be purchased for $5,000 to $15,000 and up.

❑ ❑ ❑

Q. Are articles from contributors hard to come by?
A. Most newsletter editors say they usually receive sufficient copy. "Printing Association of Florida Newsletter," a SIG publication, for example, screens a flood of incoming information to select items of possible interest to members. Generally, the newsletter receives more than enough copy for each issue.

❑ ❑ ❑

CHAPTER TWO

Introduction

The Players Are Identified

This how-to book tells how to write and publish better newsletters. It gives specific steps for producing and upgrading newsletters and brings these steps to life with examples from today's newsletters.

More and more people are publishing newsletters today, including many entrepreneurs. Whether you already publish (or plan to publish) a newsletter as an entrepreneur or are involved with newsletters in some other capacity, you'll benefit from the information presented in this book.

From university campuses to broadcast media, newsletters and their writers are increasingly in the news. As New York University reported in its *Bulletin* of fall 1991 classes at the School of Continuing Education, for example: "Newsletter publishing is one of the fastest-growing U.S. businesses today."

Not only are college students learning about newsletters, but many of today's junior and senior high school students regularly create their own newsletters dealing with extracurricular activities, according to educators. And on television today newsletters are referred to much more frequently than they were just five years ago. Viewers of TV programs such as WNET's "Wall Street Week," for example, regularly hear newsletters discussed.

Indeed, a view commonly held by publishers, as expressed in "InCider" Magazine, Vol. 7, Iss. 10, October 1989, is as follows: "If InCider's Desktop Publishing Contest last summer was any indication, everyone, it seems, is on a newsletter kick."

Take just one category: free newsletters. Examine the literature rack at any library or activities center and you'll find a wide assortment of newsletters — all free for the taking. And other categories of newsletters are expanding in a similar manner.

In general, today's newsletters speak with greater authority and are more credible than earlier editions. Increasingly, articles in the news media dealing with some technological advance look on the editors of specialized newsletters as authorities. And increasingly, newsletter editors are quoted as to the overall significance of the advance.

Newsletters presenting such overviews are in a good position to exercise impartiality. One reason for this is that newsletters, as narrow-focus, or niche, publications, are better qualified as impartial authorities on particular subjects and technologies. A second reason: newsletters usually carry less advertising than other publications and are less likely to be influenced by (or open to the inflence of) advertisers.

What does the future hold for newsletters? According to Frederick D. Goss, executive director of The Newsletter Publishers Association (Arlington, VA): "I believe we can look for continued growth and a continuing explosion of demand for more specialized information in concise, useable form."

> Editor's Note: Throughout the book, individual newsletters are cited to show what's noteworthy about newsletters of that type and, at the same time, to illustrate the various steps in writing and publishing a newsletter.

Throughout the book, newsletters are identified in the following manner: the first time a newsletter is mentioned (except in CHAPTER ONE), the name and location of its publisher, or publishing company, is also given. In CHAPTER ONE, only titles of newsletters are given. Readers wishing to know complete addresses of editors, writers, publishers, or others mentioned in the book, are referred to the APPENDIX.

The names of newsletters are enclosed in quotation marks — with one exception: The names of newsletters published by The Cobb Group are, at the request of the publisher, underlined instead of being enclosed in quotation marks.

What differentiates today's newsletters from those of the past? Today's newsletters have faster turnaround, more savvy in presenting complex subjects, more credibility, and greater candor in discussing the realities of the times. The various newsletter types are discussed in the following sections:

2.1 Subscription Newsletters

The subscription newsletter is the one in which people caught up with the entrepreneurial spirit are most interested. The reason, of course, is the annual subscription, which can run as high as $500 to $800 or more.

Most subscription newsletters publish highlights and advances in some particular field or technology — such as investments or computer graphics. For some people, this information is so valuable that they (or their companies) are willing to pay publishers top dollar for subscriptions to newsletters giving the information.

This demand has spawned a variety of subscription newsletters, from investment newsletters with advice on the stock market to business newsletters with specific business information. "Satellite Week," for example, published by Warren Publishing, Inc., (Washington, DC) is, according to senior editor Paul Warren, "a high-priced, low-volume, subscription newsletter." Subscribers look to "Satellite Week" for new developments in satellite communications and allied fields. "Our primary coverage," says Warren, "is the regulatory/policy area, although we cover business also."

❑ ❑ ❑

Many of the subscription newsletters published today use much the same writing style introduced by Kiplinger in his weekly newsletter in 1923. Written in terse form, subscription newsletters meet the requirements of today's busy executives and others who want concentrated, concise answers to such basic questions as: Who's involved? What's at stake? and What's ahead?

A newsletter written in just such an abbreviated style is "Control Industry Inside Report (CIIR)," a publication of Control Engineering (Des Plaines, IL). "CIIR" presents a biweekly summary of new and vital information for corporate leaders interested in control and instrumentation equipment worldwide. A typical issue of "CIIR" presents the highlights of news events at more than 65 companies and facilities —all within four pages.

"From the time we lead off each issue with mergers and acquisitions," says Felix Tancula, editor of "CIIR," "we try to keep all copy short and sweet."

Publishers of subscription newsletters are often quite specific in telling readers how they can use the information to their advantage. (After all, that's why the readers subscribed in the first place.)

2.2 Newsletters for Special-Interest Groups

Newsletters for special-interest groups (SIGs) are targeted at a particular audience; they contain information for people having a common interest. This shared interest can be almost anything from interest in computer-generated graphics (as in "Computer Graphics," published by the Association for Computing Machinery, Inc., NY, NY) ... to a love of animals (as in "The Latham Letter", published by The Latham Foundation, Alameda, CA).

> (A variation of the SIG publication is the newsletter for a group of users. The user group consists of members who own and/or use a particular piece of hardware or software.)

SIG newsletters fill a special niche, providing information not usually available elsewhere. Publishers can't charge much for these newsletters, though, because readers are accustomed to buying magazines and newspapers that are low in price. (Much of the cost of publishing magazines and newspapers is supported by the advertising they carry. If a reader were to buy a newspaper containing no advertising at all, for instance, a single issue of the paper might cost as much as seven or eight dollars, it has been estimated.)

A typical special-interest-group newsletter is "LAMALUG: The Apple COREspondent." This monthly newsletter of the Lansing Area Mac and Lisa Users Group (published by the members of the Desktop Publishing Special Interest Group [SIG], Lansing, MI) contains information about Apple products: announcements of coming events, descriptions of new software, advice on how to protect against computer viruses, and other information. "LAMALUG COREspondent" typically fields such questions as Can I take a tax deduction for the Mac that I use in my work?

❑ ❑ ❑

SIG newsletters often take up important issues of the day. Take, for instance, the newsletter "Privacy Times," published by the United States Privacy Council. As reported in the *New York Times* (January 25, 1992), the Privacy Council is made up of privacy advocates with a major concern: too much personal information is becoming available to others via computers, "smart cards," and other means. Indeed, the issue of privacy is inspiring heated debate, *The Times* reported. According to Evan Hendricks, publisher of the "Privacy Times," privacy has exploded into one of the major consumer issues of the 90s.

❑ ❑ ❑

If you want to address more than one SIG audience, it's best to have each group put out a separate newsletter —which accounts for the many publishers who put out multiple SIG newsletters. When a newsletter is successful, the groups are often tempted to issue another ... and still another. Indeed, there are many publishers today who produce 20 or more different newsletters.

One such multiple-newsletter publisher is the Association for Computing Machinery, Inc., (ACM) (New York, NY). ACM is a membership association for computing and information processing; it has more than 30 special-interest groups, each of which publishes its own newsletter covering a particular area. The SIGGRAPH special-interest group, for example, publishes "Computer Graphics," the association's SIG newsletter having the largest circulation.

"Computer Graphics" is published for the SIGGRAPH membership and the computer graphics community. A typical issue of "Computer Graphics" includes special articles, news and activities of SIGGRAPH and its local groups, executive committee minutes of SIGGRAPH, and a wide range of announcements and notices of coming events. The first issue for 1991, for example, contains four key articles: (1) profiles of candidates for the SIGGRAPH executive committee, (2) credits for slide sets representing the state-of-the-art in computer-generated images, (3) an extensive bibliography of research papers in a technical subarea of computer graphics, and (4) a set of abstracts of theses and dissertations in computer graphics. According to Steve Cunningham, SIGGRAPH director for publications and editor of "Computer Graphics," future issues will include more articles of a technical nature.

"Computer Graphics" also publishes other issues with more tightly focused content. One issue each year is devoted to the proceedings of the annual SIGGRAPH conference. This issue is considered the most highly regarded research publication in the field. Special issues, which are not sent to the general membership, contain special reports or the proceedings of smaller conferences.

ACM's SIG newsletters have a wide variety of publishing policies. "Some of our technical articles are solicited, while some are contributed," says Donna Baglio, associate director of ACM's SIG services. "Some of these articles are refereed, others are not—it depends on the individual editors. At present, all of our newsletters are published in print. Some day, though, we may also turn to electronic publishing."

> Editor's Note: Although facsimile machines have been used to a small degree in the past for publishing newsletters, expect that more faxes will be used for this purpose in the future. The reason: advanced faxes are coming out with features such as automatic document feed and delayed transmission. And now Ricoh has announced a device that will allow a standard fax machine to communicate over radio frequency channels.

Each year, ACM SIGs sponsor a variety of workshops, conferences, and symposia, which are attended by approximately 50,000 individuals. Over 15,000 pages of proceedings emanate from SIG conferences each year, and this information is often distributed in newsletters to ACM SIG members and subscribers.

❑ ❑ ❑

Some SIGs — and some SIG newsletters — focus on, or honor the accomplishments of, outstanding individuals. Thus, the Edna Hibel Society (Coral Springs, FL) celebrates the achievements of Edna Hibel: painter, lithographer, and porcelain artist. Formed just prior to 1977, the Society has a membership of about seven thousand Hibel art devotees. Members automatically receive copies of the "Edna Hibel Society Newsletter," and are enrolled as Friends of the Hibel Mueum of Art. Members also have the opportunity of participating in a variety of Hibel Society art tours and other activities.

> Editor's Note: The market for SIG newsletters may change in the future. Increasing numbers of magazines, such as Newsweek, are installing equipment for selective binding. This technology allows magazines to insert customized sections (generally paid for by subscribers) that compete with niche newsletters.

2.3 Organization, or Membership, Newsletters

Typically, organization newsletters are issued by nonprofit organizations or branches of government for their members and employees. In general, belonging to an organization entitles each member to a subscription to the newsletter.

Organization newsletters usually tell the Who, What, Where, and When of the organization. Organizations publishing such newsletters frequently fall in one of the following categories: health, education, welfare, labor, or government. Typically, organization newsletters are issued for a variety of reasons: raising funds, asking for payment of dues, telling the news of the organization, and other reasons.

Achieving the proper balance of content can indeed be a challenge for an editor of an organization newsletter.

At the same time, it's important for nonprofit organizations, particularly those in the health field, to keep in close touch with members. Take the case of the New Jersey Chapter of the Arthritis Foundation (Iselin, NJ), for example. This organization sends out 40,000 copies of "The Newsletter" to its members three times a year.

"Before putting an issue together," says Lila Roseman, editor of "The Newsletter," "we get staff input to determine which services, fund-raising events, and volunteers we want to feature. We usually have more than enough copy for each issue; in fact, it's often necessary to bump a few items."

Roseman's hardest job as editor is to achieve the right balance. "In each issue, we try to offer a diversity of articles. Some give medical information about arthritis; others have news about programs available through the New Jersey Chapter. Also, to encourage support of the Chapter, we publicize our fund-raising events and other ways our readers can help the Chapter fulfill its mission."

In April 1991, "The Newsletter" was officially recognized for achieving a balanced mixture of news: the publication was awarded second place in the 4th Annual Newsletter Contest for nonprofit organizations. In this contest — which was sponsored by Pro Bono, Inc., volunteers in public relations (Madison, NJ) — 41 newsletters were entered from throughout New Jersey. Each contestant submitted two consecutive newsletter issues, plus a two-page overview describing such essentials as (1) how input and photos are obtained and (2) what the newsletter staff has been trying to accomplish.

Contestants were asked to include in their overviews

such information as the number of people working on the newsletter and whether they've been having problems. In addition to a chance at the awards, contestants received critiques of their publications from Pro Bono. "The critiques were compiled from comments by three judges — all public relations professionals — plus volunteers," says Kris Pottharst, director of Pro Bono. A typical well-balanced mix of articles is illustrated in the Jan-Apr 1991 issue of "The Newsletter," as shown in TABLE 2-1.

In return for membership fees, members of the New Jersey Chapter receive the Foundation's magazine, "Arthritis Today." As an added benefit, members also receive "The Newsletter." (Other state chapters issue their own newsletters.)

Some organization newsletters, particularly the shorter ones, report on trends and events without mentioning any individuals by name. The newsletter, "Hudson City Trends," published by Hudson City Savings Bank (Paramus, NJ), fits this description. The May 1991 issue of "Hudson City Trends" reports on the bank's increased activity in mortgages, total deposits, and quarterly earnings. And, as is common practice among such newsletters, it encourages readers to do more business with the bank. Specifically, this issue of the newsletter outlines plans for expanding the bank's 24-hour service, and invites readers to apply for a 24-hour banking card. In addition, the Hudson City publication suggests that "this may very well be the time to buy that new home or refinance your present home at a lower rate."

TABLE 2-1. Balance of articles in Jan-Apr 1991 issue of "The Newsletter," published by the Arthritis Foundation, New Jersey Chapter.

1) News of programs and services:
   - six-week Arthritis Self-Help Course
   - Ear program to provide support/information by telephone volunteers and staff
   - coupon to send for free arthritis literature Arthritis Fitness program
   - "Living with Arthritis," a new educational video
2) News of fund-raising events:
   - The Annual TELETHON
   - the Chapter's upcoming "Dear Neighbor" fund- raising campaign, expected to reach about 30,000 people.
   - South Jersey Art Show
   - photo of "Jingle Bell Run" event
   - photo of "Art for Arthritis" luncheon/fashion show
3) Medical/Research articles:
   - NJ Chapter-supported research on arthritis and lupus
   - changing strategies for arthritis drug treatment
4) Volunteers:
   - outstanding support group leader highlighted
   - President thanks volunteers of Holiday Gift Wraps in three shopping malls
5) Administration and miscellaneous:
   - new National Year-Round Mail Program
   - new membership fee
   - Chapter Annual Meeting Notice
   - thank you to contributors ($150 or more) of major fund-raiser
   - photo with thank you to Compaq Computer Corporation for gift of PC
   - notice of bequests received

2.4 Corporate Newsletters (Inside and Outside)

Many corporations publish inside or outside newsletters — or both. The inside corporate newsletter, also known as a house organ or internal newsletter, has traditionally provided noncontroversial news of people and events in the life of the corporation. Many of today's internal corporate newsletters, however, are breaking with tradition. Indeed, a new level of corporate communications specialists thinks that company publications should reflect the new realities of life in the workplace. What's different? The current generation of corporate communicators believe that candor in newsletters is the most effective way to communicate with employees.

Announcements that once were posted on company bulletin boards now come directly to the employee's computer terminal. It's not unusual today for employees to learn about important company developments by watching the evening news on television. Even electronic beepers are being used more frequently today by such nontraditional users as expectant mothers and baby sitters. In September 1991, for example, *The New York Times* reported that "more than 11 million subscribers have bought or rented beepers, according to Telocator, a trade association for the personal communications industry." And letters to the editor that are critical of the corporation are being printed today in the company newsletter — when they wouldn't previously have passed the first level of management approval.

Communicating with employees may be the key to a company's survival in the recession, writes Adrian

Shoobs in the Dec. 2, 1991, issue of *The Record,* a daily newspaper covering much of northern New Jersey from its home in Hackensack. In *The Record's* "FYI" column, Shoobs presents the following tips from Frank Grazian, executive editor of "Communications Briefings," a business newsletter based in Camden County, NJ:

- Employers should tell workers that actions and attitudes have a major impact on profit and loss.
- Stress that it costs six times as much to get a customer as to keep one. What's more, one dissatisfied customer will let 11 other people know of his experience.
- Let employees know how their daily actions affect the company. If someone's efforts have won a large order, spread the good news.
- Eliminate the No. 1 reason workers ignore orders: poor directions. A study of 30 corporations shows that most people who fail to do a job correctly simply don't understand what they're supposed to do."

❑ ❑ ❑

Newsletters published for distribution outside the corporation are in most cases distributed internally as well. "News notes," published by Scientific Instruments (Hawthorne, NY), is an example of an outside corporate newsletter. "News notes" presents information on the company's latest instrumentation in the form of case histories, and is mailed at no charge to users and others involved with pure water analysis and environmental monitoring.

"For us," says Frank LaPerch, president of Scientific Instruments, "the big advantage of newsletters is their use of case histories. These highlight the strong points of our products and are supported by third-party quotations. Then, when our sales representatives call on prospective customers, they can use the newsletters as 'proof' of product benefits. Highlighting information in this way gives our statements greater credibility. In fact, a statement can be very powerful when it comes from a third party."

Sales reps for Scientific Instruments say that they make wide use of "news notes." "Even though copies of the newsletter are distributed by mail," says one of the company's representatives, "I always carry a supply of newsletters in my car. I don't want to run a risk that prospects may have misplaced their copies."

2.5 Miscellaneous Newsletters

A variety of formats come under the heading of miscellaneous newsletters. Included in this category are newsletters published for the well-being of the public, promotional newsletters, franchise newsletters, and others.

2.5.1 Newsletters Published for the Well-Being of the Public

One newsletter produced for the public's well-being is "HealthLetter," published every two months by AARP Pharmacy Service (Libertyville, IL) and distributed to retired persons. The August/September 1991 issue of this newsletter (5 1/4 by 8 1/2 inches; four pages) contains information on such subjects as back pain, flying with a head cold, sunglasses, and changes in nutrition labeling scheduled to become mandatory in May 1993. (Causes of low back pain and steps to recovery, as presented in "HealthLetter," are shown in TABLE 2-2.)

2.5.2 *Promotional Newsletters*

Promotional newsletters are not always what they seem. Designed to look at first glance as though they contain valuable information, they are, in fact, really sales pitches.

2.5.3 *Franchise Newsletters*

Another type of newsletter is the preprepared fran-

TABLE 2-2 Information on low back pain and steps for recovery, as presented in "HealthLetter"

Low back pain affects four out of five Americans; among its causes are:

- A sedentary lifestyle; muscles need to be strengthened by exercise.
- Osteoarthritis (deterioration of the joints)
- Osteoporosis (thinning of the bones)
- An arthritic condition
- A ruptured disk
- Muscle spasm

Steps for recovery include:

- Use of a chair that provides better back support
- Bed rest
- Better posture
- Sessions with a physical therapist
- Injection of a steroid
- Applying relaxation techniques
- Acupuncture

chise, or syndicated, newsletter. A company can purchase a supply of these preprinted publications, imprint its name and logo on the masthead, add its own message (when desired), and distribute finished newsletters to its customers. The resulting franchise newsletters provide publishers with the ability to communicate effectively with clients, while holding down publication costs.

Actually, franchise newsletters can be useful to readers (besides, they're free). Most homeowners have received newsletters containing information about lawns and landscaping — a common application of the franchise newsletter. The two-page newsletter "Turf-Tips," published by Green-a-Lawn, appears to be such a newsletter. In addition to the usual sales pitch, this newsletter also contains some useful information about lawns and gardens: an article about early spring treatment, advice on watering and crabgrass control, and a column on what to do with yard waste.

❑ ❑ ❑

But not all newsletters fit neatly in one or another of our five main classifications. Note the following uses of newsletters:

- A publisher may issue two newsletters containing the same subject matter but targeted for different audiences. Thus, "Construction Supervision & Safety Letter," a newsletter published by the Bureau of Business Practice (BBP) (Waterford, CT), provides tips on supervisory methods and techniques in a plant setting. At the same time, another newsletter published by BBP, "Dynamic Supervision — Office and Staff

Edition," deals with the same topic, but in an office setting.

- Sometimes a publisher may go a step further than this one-subject-but-two-newsletters approach by producing two entirely different types of publications — such as a newsletter and a journal — both dealing with the same subject. Pierian Press (Ann Arbor, MI), for example, publishes a variety of material for libraries. Its publications include "Library Hi Tech News," a 32-page newsletter, and "Library Hi Tech Journal," a journal that's three times as long as the newsletter.

  Editor's Note: What's noteworthy in the preceding example is this: A newsletter provides rapid dissemination of news while a journal provides the reader with information in depth.

- Some newsletters are offered to subscribers as part of a larger package. For example, the Bureau of National Affairs, Inc. (BNA) (Washington, DC), publishes "Payroll Administration Guide Newsletter," a biweekly. Included with each annual subscription to the newsletter is BNA's "Payroll Administration Guide." This guide consists of a five-binder notification and reference package for payroll managers.

  Together, the newsletter and the five binders function as an informational team, providing readers with a combination of services. The six-page newsletter alerts readers to trends and new procedures and regulations affecting payroll administration. Readers of the newsletter are kept up to date in such areas as new IRS rules, payroll seminars, and developments affecting computerized payrolls. The five BNA binders, on the other hand, contain 3,000 to 4,000 pages of in-depth information, such as easy-to-scan charts, the latest IRS forms, and information on the Fair Labor Standards Act.

- In addition to newsletter combinations such as the preceding examples, readers have a choice of in-print newsletters, on-line newsletters, and newsletters that are available both in print and on line. Readers can also obtain faxed newsletters, newsletters on diskette, and audio cassettes for the blind.

❑ ❑ ❑

2.6 Newsletters Versus Other Forms of Written Communication

The very day a book is published, it's already out of date because of the time it takes for compilation, printing, and distribution. Even a magazine, because of the lag time in putting it together, can be months behind the events being reported. The idea behind newsletters is to introduce a publication that can be issued so quickly that readers can learn about events within days of their occurrence.

Our world is changing at an ever-increasing pace: New materials, advanced technologies, and innovative discoveries confront us daily. Traditional publications such as magazines and journals simply can't keep up with the changes, but newsletters can; they're structured to communicate new ideas rapidly.

Traditionally, newsletters focus on brief news items

about people, events, and equipment. Magazines, on the other hand, publish longer, more-scholarly articles. Take, for example, two publications issued by the Notre Dame Alumni Association, Notre Dame, IN: "Alumni, the Newsletter for Notre Dame Alumni" and the "Notre Dame Magazine," published "for alumni and friends."

Published three times a year, the Notre Dame newsletter carries announcements of reunions, happenings at local Notre Dame clubs, alumni awards, and other short news items. "Notre Dame Magazine," on the other hand, has about five times as many pages as the newsletter. In addition to class notes, the magazine publishes numerous in-depth articles by professors, graduate students, freelance writers (some of whom attended Notre Dame), and other professionals. In a sense, the two Notre Dame publications go hand in hand: Look to the newsletter for an informational snack; turn to "Notre Dame Magazine" for a balanced meal.

❑ ❑ ❑

The traditional roles of newsletters are changing. For example, newsletters contain more space advertising and more in-depth articles today than they did just a few years ago. Take "The Portable Paper," a newsletter published by Thaddeus Computing, Inc., (Fairfield, IA) for instance. A recent issue of this publication allocated more than 25 percent (12 pages) of its total space (44 pages plus covers) to advertising. Another newsletter allotting a substantial amount of space to advertising — and to publication of in-depth articles as well — is the "Apple Library Users Group Newsletter," published by Apple Computer, Inc., Cupertino,

CA. Allocation of space in typical 1991 issues of this quarterly newsletter, published for users of Apple computers in libraries and information centers, is shown in TABLE 2-3.

Magazine advertising has been in a slump for several years now, but, as of May 1992, some magazine publishers say they expect a turnaround. By the mid-90s, some predict, magazines will become more profitable. An increase in advertising can also be expected for newsletters, due largely to their ability to target ads and the fact that they are starting at lower advertising ratios to begin with. (Magazines have always looked closely at their ratios of advertising pages to editorial pages. Will newsletters soon be tracking such ratios also?)

Sometimes a magazine or other publication will include one or two pages of news items under the heading, "newsletter." A single page headed "Market Newsletter," for example, is included in the June 1991 issue of "The Writer," a monthly magazine published by The Writer, Inc., (Boston, MA). "Market Newsletter"

TABLE 2-3 Allocation of space in "Apple Library Users Group Newsletters"

Percentage of Space*	Contents of Typical Issues
28	Reviews of books and software
45	Feature articles and columns
19	"Help wanted" and "help found" letters and other items
8	Advertising
100	

* Typical issues contain 125 pages

presents thumbnail news items about various book publishers: what types of books they like readers to submit, apologies for enclosing printed rejection slips with returned manuscripts, acceptance of reprint rights, and other matters.

❑ ❑ ❑

Another example of a publication setting aside space for an inner newsletter is the "Elderhostel Catalog." Published by ELDERHOSTEL (Boston, MA), the catalog describes courses and intensive study programs for older persons and is offered at colleges and universities throughout the world. The Fall 1991 issue of this catalog, for example, contains 128 pages (11 by 16 inches). Two of these pages are headed simply "Newsletter." Articles (one of them bylined) in this newsletter describe a new retirement institute, discuss Elderhosteling in Alaska and Florida, and urge senior citizens to attend one of the upcoming programs that still have openings.

❑ ❑ ❑

Sometimes a few pages are laid out to look like a newsletter but are published as an insert in a magazine. In the following instance, the National Computer Graphics Association (NCGA), located in Fairfax, VA, switched from a true newsletter to a pair of inserts placed in established industry magazines.

Until 1990, NCGA routinely published the newsletter "NCGA Forum" for members of the association. In 1990, however, "NCGA Forum" was discontinued and replaced by two news inserts. One of these inserts, "NCGA News," (a small-scale version of the earlier "NCGA Forum") is now incorporated in each issue of

Computer Graphics World (CGW), which is distributed to all NCGA members. The other insert, "NCGA CAD/CAM File," is published as part of *Designet Magazine* (formerly *MCN*). *Designet* is free to members of NCGA's CAD Society.

"While these inserts play an important role in helping our association communicate with members," says James A. Schuping, president and CEO of NCGA, "we recognize the importance of stand-alone association communications. In fact, NCGA is planning to launch a new newsletter this year that will keep us in touch with our members on a regular basis.

> Editor's Note: Although one or two pages of news items may present interesting and useful information, we do not consider such pages as "true" newsletters.

2.7 A Brief Newsletter History ... Of Sorts

Newsletters, historians tell us, go back 500 years or more. Although paper was invented in China in A.D.105, it took more than a thousand years for it to reach Europe. The rulers of Europe used writing not only to publicize themselves but also to keep themselves informed. King Henry VII, for example, relied on handwritten letters from his diplomats. In fact, many rulers depended on an exchange of newsletters for information. (A forerunner of on-line database input?)

A newsletter describing Edward III's successful efforts to regain his crown in 1471 was issued in both English and French. (A first in international circulation?)

In eighteenth-century Europe, written and printed forms of news were coming into wider use. "Nouvellistes" assembled their news into handwritten newsletters, which were widely distributed throughout the provinces for a fee, and their existence began to do away with sole dependence on spoken news. (Subscription newsletters?)

Gutenberg's letter press arrived in Spain 23 years before Columbus returned, and the letter Columbus wrote to the Spanish Court was set in type, printed, and distributed well before Columbus visited Barcelona. (A newsletter scoop?)

In America, the first newsletter is said to have been "The Boston News Letter," which reported ship arrivals and departures, as well as other commercial information. (Solicited articles?)

One disadvantage of these early newsletters is they were copied and recopied over and over, and errors sometimes crept in. (Doesn't happen today!)

CHAPTER THREE

Publishing Objectives

First Priority: Set Goals

Before you start on your newsletter, it's necessary to consider some fundamentals. If you plan to launch a newsletter, or want to upgrade an existing one, first ask yourself some key questions:

- Will your newsletter really meet the needs of your audience?
- What is the main information your readers are seeking?
- If the information is also available from other sources, how much do these other sources cost the reader?
- Who are the potential readers who will find your newsletter of value?
- Will your potential readers have to pay for the newsletter out of their own pockets, or do they work for companies who will pay for it?
- If competitive newsletters already serve the market you are aiming at, will your newsletter take a tack that's different enough that readers will

switch to your newsletter or buy yours along with the other?
- If other newsletters already serve your target market but are slow in getting out the information, will potential readers pay for your newsletter?
- Does your newsletter have "here and now" timeliness?

If your answers to the preceding questions are favorable, the next step suggested is to establish your objectives clearly in mind — and on paper.

3.1 Principal Objectives

The success of any enterprise depends largely on the objectives its founder(s) had in mind in undertaking the project. Nowhere is this more applicable, probably, than in launching a newsletter. Here, in the following sections, are some of the main objectives behind publication of newsletters.

3.1.1 Build a Profitable Business

Successful newsletters help build profits. Maybe you're an entrepreneur, writing on your own, or you may be helping a company launch a newsletter. Again, perhaps you're actively involved with newsletters in some other capacity. In any event, you can establish, or help establish, a profitable newsletter venture. If your primary objective is not to make a profit on newsletters, however, but to build your (or a company's) other business, a successful newsletter can help promote that business and bring in new customers. Indeed, newsletters are one of the most cost-effective ways of reaching the marketplace.

It's generally believed that with hard work and long hours, one can join the ranks of successful newsletter marketers. It does indeed take these ingredients, but it also takes a lot of good luck. According to Charles W. Felix, editor of the monthly "Food Protection Report (FPR)" (Leesburg, VA): "The hardest part of publishing a newsletter with meager resources is being able to market the letter in a [suitable] fashion. We at 'FPR' have a remarkable record of keeping our readers, but our record for adding new subscribers is not as good. The biggest obstacle to successfully marketing our newsletter is time ... and after that, insufficient funds."

❑ ❑ ❑

Many newsletter publishers not only produce one or more newsletters, but they also perform a variety of related activities, such as writing books, producing training material, conducting seminars, and lecturing. Dudley Lynch, editor of "Brain & Strategy," for example, not only finds time to edit this newsletter but to do other work as well: Lynch runs a small publishing and consulting company — Brain Technologies Corporation (Fort Collins, CO) — and even finds time to "write several books each decade."

❑ ❑ ❑

Increasingly, specialized information in newsletters is being used to sell a wide range of goods and services. In fact, sometimes a newsletter is successful even though it provides information about a product that's being phased out of existence by its manufacturer. Such is the case with "The Portable Paper," a newsletter providing information on software for Hewlett-Packard's HP 110 Portable, Portable PLUS, and HP 150 lines of laptop computers. "When our newsletter was first published in 1986," says Hal Goldstein, a coeditor of "The Portable Paper," "it was produced by just my wife and myself. Now it has a circulation of about 1,000 and is written and published six times a year. We now employ 15 to 16 people — people who also perform marketing and other duties. A typical issue contains 44 pages plus covers and is published by DTP using WordPerfect and a Hewlett-Packard LaserJet printer."

"What really makes 'The Portable Paper' special," says Goldstein, "is the quantity and quality of reader contribution." Information sent in by readers, according to Goldstein, is, in fact, the most valuable kind of input because it comes from everyday use.

Hewlett-Packard no longer manufactures portable computers, however, and "The Portable Paper" may gradually phase out of existence. To fill the gap, Thaddeus Computing, Inc. plans to launch "a number of other newsletters, beginning with one on the LaserJet printer."

3.1.2 Enable Clients and Potential Clients to Know You Better (and Vice Versa)

A newsletter column containing a profile of you or someone on your newsletter staff, a paragraph or two about each of the writers, and similar personal news items can help readers to know you and your associates (if you have associates) better.

Even very technical newsletters sometimes contain less-technical, human-interest editorials and articles. During the 1980s, for example, the column "Comment" was carried in all issues of "TIS News," a newsletter published by Technicon Industrial Systems (Tarrytown, NY). "Comment" regularly presented the editorial views of Technicon marketing executives, and each column was accompanied by a photograph of the author.

❑ ❑ ❑

In the initial issue of The DOS Authority, publisher Douglas Cobb told readers that they now had at their fingertips a wealth of timesaving ways to use DOS more efficiently. The DOS Authority, a monthly publication of The Cobb Group (Louisville, KY), provides tips and techniques for advanced users of MS-DOS and PC-DOS operating systems that control personal computers. "My goal," says Cobb, "is to make this publication one of the most useful on the reference shelf. I encourage you to send in your comments, criticisms, suggestions, and ideas for articles you would like to see published."

Then, to make it easy for readers to respond, a postage-paid reply card is included as part of the newsletter. In the initial issue, reply cards enabled readers to rate seven articles, five of which were written by outside writers. Readers were asked to rate each article in terms of three questions: Is it useful? Is it interesting? Is it clearly presented? (Refer to FIGURE 3-1)

3.1.3 Build Lists of Satisfied Readers and Satisfied Users

Well-written newsletters can result in both satisfied readers and satisfied users. Customer satisfaction is vitally important for any company that is marketing a product or service. If, for example, you are writing for a corporate newsletter that publishes case histories, you will find as time passes that the succession of users

RATINGS!

Rate This Issue!

THE DOS AUTHORITY™

Article	Useful topic?	Interesting topic?	Clearly presented?
Keeping track of the current drive and directory	Yes No	Yes No	Yes No
Smashing the 640K barrier	Yes No	Yes No	Yes No
Handling multiple configurations with AUTOEXEC...	Yes No	Yes No	Yes No
Safeguard your AUTOEXEC.BAT file	Yes No	Yes No	Yes No
How DOS handles hard disk partitions	Yes No	Yes No	Yes No
Using the SHELL statement to activate...	Yes No	Yes No	Yes No
Testing for case using the FOR statement	Yes No	Yes No	Yes No

Your overall opinion of this issue Great OK Poor

Comments/Ideas ______________________________

Name ______________________ Phone (____) ______________

Q 2031 3-91

FIGURE 3-1 Reply card in premier issue of The DOS Authority. Readers were invited to rate articles.

thus written up constitutes a practical and useful list of satisfied users.

3.1.4 If You're Writing for a Company, Your Newsletter Can Reinforce the Company's Messages

Newsletters are frequently used to announce company seminars and other coming events, solicit articles for the newsletter, or call readers' attention to some product feature or problem. Newsletters can also be used, for example, to highlight the annual report or explain the rationale of a company merger or other development.

3.1.5 Identify Hot Sales Prospects

Hot sales prospects can be effectively identified through the use of reply cards or reader service cards. For example, mailing out reply cards can provide valuable information on users' intent to buy (see CHAPTER TWELVE).

3.1.6 Send Newsletters to Names on Rented Lists, Based on Contents of Each Issue

By renting names and addresses, and marking identifying codes on reply cards mailed out with your newsletters, new subscribers or readers can be gained for your newsletter.

For many years, Technicon Industrial Systems published five different newsletters. Generally, one or two lists of names and addresses were rented for distribution of each issue. Lists were selected on the basis of the contents of individual newsletter issues; thus, a list of power industry executives, for example, would be purchased and used to mail out an issue containing a case history article on Con Edison.

3.1.7 Announce New Products or Services

Announcements of new software or new models of equipment can be published in regular issues of your newsletter. Even if the request to publish such information comes to you between regular issues, however, a special edition of your newsletter can be quickly issued. Newsletters offer a convenient way to announce special sales; readers can be notified that a particular piece of software, say, is being given away free to anyone purchasing a new model of equipment.

3.1.8 Establish an Ongoing Relationship with Your Readers

From your very first issue, you can establish a two-way flow of communication with your readers. "Network Consultant Quarterly" (NCQ), a newsletter in the field of telecommunications, typifies how this can be accomplished. When this newsletter sought feedback from readers, the following simple editorial was inserted in the Editor's Corner of the Summer 1990 issue:

> Response to the "Network Consultant Quarterly" has been overwhelming. Since the first issue was published in 1987, it has been an unbiased source for technology and application information. The editor welcomes comments or suggestions about past or future issues, industry topics, special-interest groups, or other topics that would greater enhance the effectiveness of this program. In the U.S., call ....

❑ ❑ ❑

Reply cards also promote two-way communication. When sent out with newsletters, they provide a convenient way for readers to express their opinions of your publication.

3.1.9 Equip Sales Representatives with a Useful Sales Aid

Newsletters, especially those containing case histories, are particularly useful to sales representatives.

3.2 Secondary Objectives

Although the following objectives are, in general, less important than the principal objectives, there are specific instances where these secondary objectives are very important indeed.

3.2.1 Update Readers with New Information, Such as Technological Advances and Revisions to Instruction Manuals

Many newsletter publishers depend on the flexibility of newsletters to disseminate information more quickly than other print media. The publisher of "Offline," an in-house newsletter issued for staff members by the Tacoma Public Library (TPL) (Tacoma, WA), confirms this to be the case. "Offline" highlights problem areas, policy changes, and new developments in the field of library science. Although much of the material eventually finds its way into manual rewrites, members of "Offline" say, its importance requires immediate dissemination, sometimes in graphic detail.

❑ ❑ ❑

Another example is found in "Water News," published by Virginia Water Resources Research Center at Virginia Polytechnic Institute and State University (Blacksburg, VA).

Take the lead article in the March 1992 issue, for example. Elizabeth B. Crumbley, editor of "Water News," has this to say on the benefit of rapid publication of newsletters:

"This lead article [discusses] legislation in our General Assembly. I try to cover the assembly so that our readers can have time to find out about water resource proposals and react to them while their assembly represtatives are still deliberating."

To be sure, nowhere can readers obtain more timely, specific information than in newsletters. (It's no wonder that subscribers are willing to pay large sums for subscriptions to some newsletters.)

❑ ❑ ❑

Newsletters are well suited to the task of updating readers on key issues of the day. Consider the American Dental Association's tabloid newsletter "ADA News," for example, which is published semimonthly (except for July and December, when it's published once each month) by ADA Publishers, Inc. (Chicago, IL).

The April 6, 1992, issue of "ADA News" provided readers with up-to-date information on standards and regulations of the Occupational Safety and Health Administration (OSHA) — a subject of much importance to readers. This particular issue of the newsletter, for example, included the following information relating to OSHA standards:

- Suggestions were published for readers who have "decided that hiring a health and safety consultant is the best way to ensure that their dental office complies with all OSHA regulations."
- A checklist was included for readers to follow before making a final decision on which consultant to hire. Using the checklist, for example, readers could check such matters as "whether the consultant is knowledgeable about OSHA regulations, realizes a dental office is different from an industrial worksite, charges a fair price, and will deliver as promised."
- Also included was a list of the 20 most common citations OSHA issued to dentists in federal OSHA-plan states between January 1990 and Oc-

tober 1991. Among the citations listed were the following: "violations in labeling containers containing hazardous chemicals ... and violations of the standard requiring biohazard warning signs."

- Also presented in this issue of "ADA News" was information on the 1992 ADA Public Affairs Conference, where nearly 300 state and national dental leaders discussed important issues, including "OSHA's bloodborne disease standard, national health policy, OSHA regulations," and other topics.

❑ ❑ ❑

Another benefit of rapid publication of newsletters is that, in addition to providing an efficient and timely way to notify readers about scheduled events, they also provide a time-saving way for readers to register for those events. One special-interest-group newsletter containing information on coming events is "Water News." The March 1992 issue of "Water News" describes several conferences and seminars scheduled for the coming month. One of these events, for instance, was the Virginia Water Resources Conference, at which topics from wetlands mitigation to stormwater regulations were covered. For readers wishing to attend, "Water News" even included a registration form at the back of the newsletter.

Keep in mind, though, that many newsletters contain information that's so complex it doesn't make sense to readers unless they are directly involved with the particular technology. Developments in library science, software, and on-line databases, for example, are best understood by readers having hands-on experience with these technologies.

❑ ❑ ❑

Sometimes notices of price increases are transmitted via newsletter. In its first issue of 1991, for example, "The Newsletter" of the New Jersey Chapter of the Arthritis Foundation notified readers that minimum Chapter membership dues would increase to $20 (from $15) to support publication of *Arthritis Today*, the national magazine and membership benefit.

3.2.2 Invite Readers to Make Suggestions

Newsletters offer a convenient way for readers to make suggestions; users sometimes report novel uses for a product.

When the DuPont Company (Wilmington, DE) launched an instrument venture in the early 1960s, the newly formed division introduced "The Thermogram," a quarterly newsletter reporting happenings in the field of thermal analysis. Reader response was very favorable, but even more than that, many readers unexpectedly returned reply cards telling of a variety of applications for DuPont thermal analyzers —important information that DuPont management had only in part.

3.2.3 Encourage Readers to Buy a Product Before a Price Increase Goes into Effect

Newsletters can be published so quickly these days that they are ideal for disseminating such information as the availability of a product or service at a lower price and for a specified period of time.

3.2.4 Open Doors that Might Otherwise Remain Closed

Newsletters are effective door-openers. Since they can be produced rapidly, they are often the first to communicate important news, opening doors that might otherwise remain closed. At times, doors are opened merely by mailing the appropriate newsletter issue. At other times, a sales representative trying to reach someone in an unresponsive account may use a newsletter article about a competitor of the account as an opening wedge.

3.2.5 Establish Yourself and Your Newsletter as Experts in Your Field

To an increasing degree, news media reporting on new developments or technologies include in their articles an impartial overview of the development. Sometimes this overview comes from an independent spokesman, such as a member of a trade association. At other times, a newsletter that is especially knowledgeable on the subject is quoted. When, for example, *The New York Times* published an article in November 1991 about IBM's pact with the Intel Corporation to jointly design computer chips for PCs, a newsletter publisher was quoted on the significance of this news. (The pact, reported *The Times*, gave IBM the right to buy Intel's chips first; it also allowed IBM to modify them.) According to Michael Slater, the publisher of "Microprocessor Report," an industry newsletter, the pact gave "IBM the flexibility to build things the other guys don't have."

❑ ❑ ❑

Who knows, if things go well with your newsletter,

you may even become known as an expert some day. Take "The Kiplinger Washington Letter," for example. Published by The Kiplinger Washington Editors, Inc., (Washington DC), it's one of the first, if not the first, subscription newsletter. Circulated weekly to business clients since 1923, the Letter is widely known in the publishing field. In fact, many of today's subscription newsletters use the Letter's well-known editorial style and handling of content. Indeed, extensive use of forecasts, abbreviated sentence structure, underlining, and frequent use of ellipses (...) have become hallmarks of this type of newsletter. The following excerpts from the "The Kiplinger Washington Letter" of May 10, 1991, are typical:

> Exports ... smaller gains ahead as overseas economies slow further.
>
> Hardly any boost from gov't spending ... budget strains everywhere.

3.3 Update Your Objectives

As your newsletter — or your plan for launching one — matures, your objectives will no doubt shift also. Consider, for example, the changes made at the newsletter "Brain & Strategy":

"Our objectives have changed considerably since the first issue of our newsletter was published in 1982," says Dudley Lynch, who serves as editor and does most of the work of putting each issue together. "The format has been revised several times. Even the title has changed from 'Teleido Letter' to 'Creativity Letter' to 'Brain & Strategy.' Now, 'DolphinThinks Brain & Strategy Newsletter' is frequently used as our title. Our thinking, too, has changed, although the basic theme of the newsletter — changing creativity in a business or organizational context — remains the same."

3.4 After Your Objectives Have Been Established, Focus on Topics

Once your objectives have been clearly defined, it's a good idea to accumulate a list of topics (with outlines) that will appear in the first several issues of your newsletter. This way, you will not only get a start on writing newsletter issues to come, but will get further indication of whether your venture is indeed likely to be successful.

CHAPTER FOUR

Basic Considerations

A Look at Fundamentals

As you move ahead with your newsletter plans, there are many things to think about. CHAPTER FOUR discusses some basic considerations that should be addressed early on.

4.1 Establish Newsletter Size and Format

Newsletters vary widely in size, depending on the particular communications task. Some are as short as one or two pages; others are as long as the Library of Michigan's "Access" (8 1/2 by 11 inches, 126 pages.)

Newsletter lengths most frequently used are two pages (one 8 1/2 by 11 sheet), four pages (one 11 by 17 sheet), and eight pages (two 11 by 17 sheets). All of these sizes can be produced without the need for staples. (To accommodate small page size, a combination of software such as Publish It! 2 and AppleWorks Classic can be used effectively.)

Successful publications tend to grow in size and

circulation over the years. Take the "Printing Association of Florida Newsletter," for example, which is published 11 times a year by the Printing Association of Florida, Inc. (PAF) (Southern Region: Hialeah, FL; Northern Region: Orlando, FL)

"We screen a flood of incoming information to select items of possible interest to members," says Gene Strul, editor of "Printing Association of Florida Newsletter." "We usually receive more than enough copy; our newsletter is 16 pages long now, but we anticipate going to 24 pages soon."

> Editor's Note: Although the newsletters we have seen range from 2 to 126 pages in length, most are well inside these extremes.

One way of adding pages to a newsletter without fouling up the numbering of the original pages is the method occasionally used by the eight-page "Food Protection Report." A four-page "Inside Report" is inserted between pages 4 and 5 (and numbered 4A, 4B, 4C, and 4D), thus increasing the total number of pages in the newsletter by 50 percent.

To simplify newsletter layout and pasteup (especially where some of the work is performed by part-time employees or volunteers), you may want to use forms that help establish margins, column widths, and other parameters of the printed page. Pads of these forms (with invisible blue-ink guidelines and other information) can be obtained from a supplier such as Communication Resources, North Canton, OH — or from most large stationers.

4.2 Select a Title (and Possibly a Subtitle)

In deciding on a title for your newsletter, it's advantageous that it describe either the newsletter's subject matter or its target audience — or both. For example, the newsletter "Moneysworth" prospered and eventually became a magazine when its circulation grew to more than half a million. Its catchy title probably helped to boost sales.

❑ ❑ ❑

It's also recommended that your title be clever ... if possible. Newsletters such as "mixin'" (American Bartender's Association), "The Migrant" (Michigan Audubon Society), and "New Waves" (Texas Water Resources Institute-Texas A&M University) are typical eye-catching titles that also provide an indication of content. A newsletter's title, however, is not always indicative of its contents.

Although most newsletters do not have subtitles, these secondary identifications, when used, help clarify abbreviated or cryptic newsletter titles. Thus, the newsletter ".dbf," is accompanied by the subtitle "The authoritative dBase monthly." Typical subtitles used by newsletters are shown in TABLE 4-1.

4.3 Identify Issues

For identification purposes, you may want to print Vol., No., and Date on each issue, as done by "Atex Times," a newsletter published by Atex Inc., Billerica, MA.

To achieve greater publishing flexibility (by not

TABLE 4-1 Newsletter subtitles

Newsletter	Subtitle
"Ada Letters"	A Bimonthly Publication of SIGAda, the ACM Special-Interest Group on Ada
"Atex Times"	An Employee Publication of Atex, Inc.
"Brain & Strategy"	Business Intelligence on the Cutting Edges of Change
".dbf"	The authoritative dBase monthly
"Food Protection Report"	The Monthly Report of Current Developments in Food Protection
"Library Link"	For State Government Employees From the Library of Michigan
"Perspective"	News from the Library of Michigan Service for the Blind and Physically Handicapped
"Reference (Clipper)"	THE INDEPENDENT GUIDE TO CLIPPER EXPERTISE
"The Quick Answer"	The independent monthly guide to Q&A expertise

committing yourself in advance to a specific publishing date), however, you may want to print just No. and Date, as done by the newsletter "Library Hi-Tech News." Or you may prefer to simply use Date by itself, as done by "Alumni," the newsletter for Notre Dame alumni.

By identifying each issue — such as by printing Vol., No., and Date — and by mailing out copies according to a set schedule, readers will be more inclined to look forward to receiving future issues. If, in addition, you include footnotes and references for any major articles, the level of your newsletter will be even further enhanced in the eyes of readers. In some instances, readers may even cite your newsletter in their own publications, giving your newsletter added credibility.

4.4 Set Standards for Type: Underlining, Boldface, Italics, and Other Parameters

Uniformity improves the readability of a newsletter. (Refer to CHAPTER NINE: Improve Newletter Uniformity with a Stylebook.)

4.5 Choose Between Self-Mailer and Mailing in Envelope

Various forms of self-mailers are shown in TABLE 4-2

Self-mailers may take any of several different forms. One arrangement that's well suited for newsletters that are approximately 8 1/2 by 11 inches in size and up to about 12 pages in length is to print an integral, franked reply card at the bottom (or top) of the last page. The

TABLE 4-2. Various forms of self-mailers

Form of Self-Mailer	Newsletter
Size 17 by 11 inch sheet, folded to 8 1/2 by 11 inches and mailed bulk rate without an envelope	"DUN'S DATALINE"
Sealed with heavy-duty staple	"NEWSLETTER"
Sealed with wafer of tape	"TIS NEWS"

newsletter is then folded to the size of a #10 envelope and sealed with a wafer of tape.

A variation of this arrangement is to print a separate reply card, which is tipped into the newsletter before sealing.

Another arrangement is that used to send out the "NEWSLETTER," a monthly newsletter for members of the Retired United Pilots Association (RUPA). The "NEWSLETTER" — a 5 1/2 by 8 1/2 inch booklet, 60 pages in length — is closed with a single heavy-duty staple. Each issue weighs three ounces, is mailed first class, and, according to RUPA, costs the association approximately $20 per member per year to produce and mail.

Readers of the RUPA newsletter are advised that "RUPA has never sent bills or statements...nor does it require $20 annually from each member. Remit whatever makes you feel comfortable. Any amount, sent annually, entitles you to the 'NEWSLETTER.'" Although most members contribute $20 each year, others send in even more.

Most members of RUPA are retired United pilots; some are dispatchers. Members are invited to submit brief communications (letters or articles) to the publication each year in their birth month. (Instructions for submitting these communications are minimal: typed copy preferred, but hand-written copy acceptable. Width not to exceed six inches.) These contributed pieces from members are printed in the "NEWSLETTER" booklet, two to four on a page, along with other information, such as highlights of the RUPA Convention.

❑ ❑ ❑

Self-mailed newsletters take any of several different forms, depending on size and number of pages, any preferences of the publisher, and other considerations. Although self-mailers are not as common today as they once were, they do offer several advantages. Take the case of "TIS NEWS," newsletters published by Technicon Industrial Systems (Tarrytown, NY). During the 1970s and 80s, five quarterly Technicon newsletters, each having a circulation of between 10,000 and 25,000, were distributed as self-mailers via first class mail. These mailings, all containing reply cards, received high rates of response and were considered very successful.

4.6 Registering a Copyright; Protecting against Reproduction; And Quoting without Permission

Under some circumstances you will be glad to have others quote from your newsletter — with, or even without, your permission. Under most circumstances, however, it's wise to file an application for copyright registration in the Copyright Office.

Full information on registering a copyright can be obtained at no charge by writing to:

Register of Copyrights
Copyright Office
Library of Congress
Washington, DC 20559

In general, the following information applies to copyrights:

- An application can be filed by sending a nonrefundable filing fee (usually $20), a completed application form, and a nonreturnable copy of one issue of your newsletter to the above address.
- Copyright fees are adjusted every five years; the next adjustment is due in 1995.
- After your application has been acted upon, you will be able to announce your copyright by printing ©, the date (the year of first publication of your newsletter), and your name or the name of the owner of your newsletter.
  © 1992 Bill Smith
  If you prefer, the word "copyright" can be used in place of C in a circle. Thus:
  Copyright 1992 Bill Smith
- Although you cannot copyright the title of your newsletter, you can copyright the graphic presentation, or design, of that title in your logo.
- To use material copyrighted by others, you must first obtain the owner's written permission.

Here in part is what some typical newsletters say (or don't say) about copyrights and using information from other newsletters:

- "Apple Library Users Group Newsletter" states:

  "© 1990 ... Material may be reprinted with permission."

- "Printing Association of Florida Newsletter," previously known as "GraphicsUpdate," a newsletter published by the Printing Association of Florida, Inc., stated:

  "Published by the members of the Printing Association of Florida, Inc. (PAF) with the permission of Graphic Communications World and the American Institute of Certified Public Accountants for their contributions to this newsletter. All rights reserved."

- Most newsletters indicate that their material cannot be quoted without permission. Some, however, would like to have their copy quoted as widely as possible; these newsletters often state that permission to quote from their publication is not required. One newsletter giving open permission is the 12-page "Food Protection Report" (FPR), published monthly by Charles Felix Associates:

  "Subscribers and media," states FPR, "may quote from contents, crediting source."

4.7 When Should Your Logo Be Printed on Each Page of the Newsletter?

Sometimes it's essential to print your logo on each page of your newsletter; at other times it's optional. If you're working on a subscription newsletter, or a newsletter to a special-interest group, it's important to print the title of your newsletter, together with your logo or the name of your company, on each page. That way, anyone tempted to use your copy without permission will always be reminded that the copy belongs to you.

Even if you're working on a newsletter that contains no coprighted or proprietary information (such as a corporate or organization newsletter), you may still want your logo and the title of the newsletter to appear on each page. Why? Either because you want the publicity or you want to make sure no one else receives credit for your information.

4.8 How Often Will You Publish?

Publishing frequencies of most newsletters range from weekly to quarterly distribution. Typical frequencies are shown in TABLE 4-3.

4.9 How Will the Newsletter Be Printed?

Will the newsletter be set in type? Will a word processor or desktop publishing be used? (Refer to CHAPTERS TEN and ELEVEN.)

TABLE 4-3 Publishing frequencies of newsletters

Publishing Frequency	Newsletter
Weekly	"Television Digest" "The Kiplinger Washington Letter"
Monthly	"COSMEP newsletter" "Food Protection Report" "foxtalk" "Smart Times" "Water News"
11 times a year	"The TImes," published 11 times a year for the Santa Clara Valley TIPC Users Group
8 to 10 times a year	"Brain & Strategy" "Online Newsletter"
Every 2 Months	"Ada Letters" (Six times a year with the exception of special issues covering workshop procedures)
Quarterly	"Apple Library Users Group Newsletter" "Network Consultant Quarterly" "Perspective" "The Latham Letter"

4.10 Consider Offering Back Issues

After your newsletter becomes established and you're publishing issues with regularity, you may want to offer readers copies of back issues. You may decide to supply previous issues free of charge — or charge your standard price for single issues (if you've established such a price). Even if you decide not to offer back issues at this time, though, experience has shown that it may pay to print an extra hundred or so copies of each issue just in case you later change your mind.

4.11 Encouraging Readers to Retain Back Issues

If you want to encourage readers to keep copies of your newsletter in a 3-ring binder, either punch holes before making distribution, or leave space in the margin so readers can punch holes later.

4.12 How Much Will You Charge for a Subscription Newsletter?

Annual subscriptions vary widely. At or near the high end are the growing number of newsletters being used to communicate specialized information, such as on emerging technologies. It's frequently more effective and more profitable to publish a high-priced newsletter for a limited market than a low-priced newsletter for a broad market.

Then, too, don't forget mailing costs; they can add up quickly. Some newsletters, such as "Printing Association of Florida Newsletter" (typically 16 pages per issue), are distributed by bulk mail, but most are sent by first class mail.

Some typical annual subscriptions are listed in TABLE 4-4.

TABLE 4-4. Some typical newsletter subscriptions

Newsletter	Total Circ.	How Often Published	Yearly Subscription
"Control Industry Inside Report"	1100	twice monthly	$125
"Food Protection Report"	na	monthly	125
"Metals Weekly"	—	weekly	700
"Satellite Week"	na	weekly	598
"Science Watch"	500*	11/year	295
"The Portable Paper"	1600	bimonthly	**

* First year
** Included in membership; $55 for non-members

4.13 Consider Advertising

Although most newsletters do not carry advertisements, those that do advertise vary widely in their use of ads. "GraphicsUpdate," now the "Printing Association of Florida Newsletter," typically carried three kinds of advertising: display ads, classified ads, and, on two pages at the back of the 16-page newsletter, an Advertising Directory of Printing Services.

Critics sometimes raise an eyebrow if a newsletter

carries paid advertising. No one objects, though, when a magazine runs an ad — and there is really no reason for anyone to object to a newsletter carrying paid advertising.

4.14 Subscription Fulfillment and Renewal if Newsletter Is Discontinued

When a newsletter ceases publication and the business is sold, what does its editor do about unfulfilled subscriptions? It's common practice in the field of publishing for a publication acquiring the assets of a defunct publisher to fulfill any of its outstanding subscription terms. "The Business Week Newsletter for Information Executives," published until mid-1990 by the Management Information Center of McGraw-Hill, Inc., used a slight variation of this accepted fulfillment practice. When, because of market conditions, the McGraw-Hill newsletter was discontinued, readers were offered a choice of another McGraw-Hill publication or one from a different publisher.

❑ ❑ ❑

Another newsletter which went out of business was "The SenTInel." It had been published to serve the entire Texas Instruments Professional Computer (TIPC) community. (At one time there were more than 20 such user groups, but Texas Instruments' Professional Computers dropped in popularity, and the number of user-groups decreased.) When illness and a declining newsletter circulation forced the editor, Dick Mitch, to stop publishing, he arranged for Thor Firing, editor of "The TImes," to print and mail enough additional copies of "The Times" to cover the unfilled obligations of the "The SenTInel." ("The TImes" is a similar newsletter for a different user group: The Santa Clara Valley TIPC Users Group.)

In the TImes's summary of services to members, editor Firing discusses the valuable assistance provided by groups of users. Firing points out that the "essence of user-group utility is mutual support. Through the newsletter, we share with users all over the country the tips and tricks that improve the usefulness of our machines. Input may be furnished either on hard copy or on disk, the latter preferred. If on disk, please use either WordPerfect, plain ASCII, or WordStar format, in that order of preference. In terms of technical support, the collective experience of members offers the likelihood of reliable answers to many of the common problems encountered by users."

CHAPTER FIVE

Information Sources

"Garbage In — Garbage Out" Applies to Newsletters, Too

5.1 Prepare Input for Your Newsletter

No newsletter is ever better than its sources of information. This probably explains why writers and editors of newsletters are always on the lookout for the ideal information source. The principal sources of input include company news releases, product announcements, interviews, on-line and CD-ROM databases, and letters to the editor. Important input is also provided by various types of written articles, including contributed articles, book reviews, software appraisals, solicited articles, and case histories. If you're writing for a company that conducts significant amounts of research and development, its R&D effort can often be a source of useful information.

> Editor's Note: Remember, though, that most of the information you obtain from outside sources — such as book reviews, case histories, and even

brief interviews — must eventually be signed off. It can complicate your writing life if you have to deal with too many sign-offs at the same time — in contrast to using input that you generate on your own.

Before information can be used in a newsletter, however, certain steps must be taken to prepare the copy. Take the case of Pinnacle Publishing, Inc. (Kent, WA), for example. As of May 1992, Pinnacle produced seven subscription newsletters dealing with the database programs of various software manufacturers. In its newsletters, Pinnacle makes wide use of case studies in which freelance authors tell how they use database programs. Pinnacle's procedure for gathering input is as follows: technical editors in the field receive contributed articles in Microsoft Word or ASCII format — and pass them along to staff, or in-house, editors. After being reviewed by the staff editors, articles are returned to the technical editors, who either approve the copy or return it to the authors for revision and sign-off.

Usually, Pinnacle newsletters are either 16 or 24 pages in length, and contributed articles can run as long as eight or more pages. To achieve some measure of uniformity among articles, Pinnacle issues writer's guidelines to its freelance authors. (After publication, the authors are paid honoraria.)

Pinnacle's style base is its newsletter, "Reference (Clipper)": initial capitals, all boldface, and no quotation marks. "Reference (Clipper)" deals with Clipper, a database program manufactured by Nantucket Corp. What distinguishes "Reference (Clipper)," says Charles Bestor, senior editor for Pinnacle, is that it's an application-development tool. That is, it's used to program applications which are then sold or given to other users. Each issue of "Reference (Clipper)" contains about half a dozen bylined articles. The April 1991 issue, for example, presents articles on building a menu, adding picture clauses to TBrowse columns, preventing index corruption, establishing security, and building data collections.

❑ ❑ ❑

Whenever there's a possibility that editing may have changed the sense of an article, editors frequently send copy back to the authors for approval. At the Library of Michigan, for example, "Access" and other newsletters often contain book reviews and articles by outside authors. "We simply scan the authors' material into whatever format is being used for the particular publication," says John Rummel, the Library's Public Information Officer and publications editor. After scanning, copy is edited...and faxed to the authors for approval.

"This is the reverse of what one would normally expect," explains Rummel. "Two factors account for this: (1) the editing process usually shortens the piece, and (2) while electronic scanners are better now than they used to be, authors still strike over characters or write in changes at times, causing sensors to read the manuscript incorrectly."

❑ ❑ ❑

Editors may also return copy to authors for approval when an article deals with a brand-new technology. Notice, for example, how this is handled at "Network Consultant Quarterly," a newsletter launched in 1987 and now published four times a year by Telematics

International Inc. (Fort Lauderdale, FL). This newsletter publishes information about new technologies in the field of communications, from a vendor-independent consultant viewpoint.

"Generally," says Ned Stirlen, editor of "Network Consultant Quarterly," "we take a single topic and discuss it in depth in three or four articles, or case studies, in a given issue. One of these articles usually presents a Telematics application. Whenever we publish an article dealing with an emerging technology, we automatically request the author's approval of the edited material. Such was the case, for instance, in our Winter 1989 issue, where articles appeared on frame relay — a new packet-switching technology. High-speed frame relay technology hadn't even been fully defined at the time, so sign-offs were required from the writers."

❑ ❑ ❑

An entirely different approach to gathering input is that taken by the newsletter "View from the Ledge." The approach is unique: clippings gathered from publications. Yes, clippings of stories (even just headlines) that are "funny or ironic or weird — yet are also true," are used by Chuck Shepherd (Washington, DC) in publishing his newsletter.

"If something is genuinely strange," says Shepherd, "you don't need to add a thing. You just put in enough information so the reader can admire its authenticity." Shepherd receives about two dozen letters and clippings a day. In fact, the only way to get on the mailing list for Shepherd's newsletter is to send in clippings.

"View from the Ledge," typically four 8 1/2 X 11 pages, was introduced in 1981. The main objective in launching the newsletter was "fun," according to Shepherd. The newsletter now has a circulation of 1,200 and is published "for the editor's friends and kindred spirits." In publishing "View from the Ledge," says Shepherd, he has "all the problems and joys of any hobbyist."

❑ ❑ ❑

Another useful source of input for newsletters is the letter to the editor. Take "The Portable Paper," for example. A typical issue of this newsletter consists of 42 pages and contains about 10 letters to the editor. In general, the letters contain information that may be useful to other readers. For example, some letters ask for help with instrument problems; others describe applications or new wrinkles of the equipment.

5.1.1 Obtain Source Material from On-Line Databases or CD-ROM (Where Appropriate)

More and more frequently, on-line databases and CD-ROM are being used to gather input for newsletters.

What's a database? It's merely a collection of information, organized alphabetically. A telephone directory is a database, for example, and so is a card catalog in the library. These are both known as flat-field databases, because all the information about a particular individual is on one line of the phone directory — or all the information about a particular book is, in most cases, on a single library card.

Flat-field databases are widely used in computer programs, such as programs to keep address books up-to-date or to make a list of appointments.

Relational databases, on the other hand, are quite different. Although they may retain the same information as flat-field databases, they hold it in separate collections, where the user can make greater use of the information.

Let's suppose that you want a list of all newsletters published in ZIP CODE 07627, or all free newsletters dealing with biology or genetics that are located in the New York City area. Relational databases can quickly answer your needs.

❑ ❑ ❑

Take the Greenwood Publishing Group of Westport, CT, for example. Its procedure for handling queries was reported in the *New York Times* on Oct. 8, 1991:

"Greenwood has 20,000 titles and processes over 40,000 orders per year. They needed high processing speed and relational database capabilities for swift response to customer queries about authors and titles. A solution integrating order processing, inventory control, royalty accounting, and financial management gave them the happy ending they were hoping for."

❑ ❑ ❑

More than 3,000 on-line databases can be reached today via modem and personal computer. Databases can be accessed by either of two routes:

(1) Database companies such as Dialog, BRS, and DataStar serve as gateways to other databases.

(2) Database companies also publish manuals listing the various databases.

On-line databases tell you how much information a particular search can provide so you will know how much information is available. This will help you in laying out your newsletter. On-line databases also provide an easy way to communicate with others.

Indeed, people having common interests are able to send messages back and forth by means of electronic bulletin boards and electronic mail.

Some on-line database services charge both by the hour and by the number of citations retrieved from the database. It's important, therefore, to know how to extract the correct information quickly and efficiently. People working with databases on a regular basis — such as corporate librarians and independent on-line researchers — usually know how to zero in on the right database without any delay, but less-experienced hands can use up costly service time. Unfortunately, database titles don't always indicate what they contain.

Among the major computer-information services in the U.S. is Prodigy, which is operated as a joint venture by International Business Machines Corporation and Sears, Roebuck & Company. Prodigy introduced its service nationally in 1990, and by mid-1991 was reported to have signed up more than 550,000 members. Other database services include Compuserve, Genie, Quantum, and America On-line. If you are writing about a national event — such as a presidential election or a wetlands issue — database services can furnish up-to-the-minute information.

"The Record," a daily newspaper in Bergen County, New Jersey, has the state's largest electronic database available to the public. Subscribers to this service, arranged through Data Times or Vu/Text, have instant access to stories published in "The Record." All that's required is a computer terminal or keyboard and a communications modem.

Among the many newsletters using database input is "Dun's Dataline," published by Dun's Marketing

Services, a Company of the Dun & Bradstreet Corporation (Parsippany, NJ). "Dun's Dataline" is published for its customers worldwide, providing information about Dun & Bradstreet's databases on Dialog. (Dialog has over 380 databases.)

> Editor's Note: On-line database companies sometimes charge as much as $250 per hour, so it pays to define the specific information you need before starting an actual search.

❑ ❑ ❑

Much the same information can be obtained using on-line CD-ROM (compact disk; read-only memory). Simply insert a compact disk (like the familiar audio disk) into a holder and place the holder in a CD-ROM drive. One compact disk holds a tremendous amount of information: over 600 megabytes, the equivalent of approximately 250,000 pages of text.

5.2 Jump-Start Your Newsletter with a Case History

An important source of input for newsletters is the interview; in fact, the ensuing case history article is often the most telling news item in the newsletter. Case histories can be as long as five or six pages — or as short as a paragraph or two. The case history is the mainspring of the newsletter, and information is presented here on how to write them successfully. Specifically, CHAPTER FIVE discusses the various steps involved in coming up with full-length case history articles. (The information will also be useful to writers of shorter articles.)

What's involved in writing a case history? Although

case histories are closely related to other forms of technical writing, such as the profile and the science article, turning out successful case histories calls for a different approach than producing other forms of communication.

Case histories, by definition, deal with individuals and their use of products or software or information. In writing a case history, it's important that the user — the customer who is making advantageous use of a specific product — be fully satisfied with the final write-up. This is essential because after the newsletter is published, the user — the protagonist of your case history — is likely to wind up being a third-party reference for the very product described. Clearly, it's important to the company marketing the product that the user speak about it favorably — both in the case history and in person.

Initially, case histories were used in two disciplines: medicine and social work. Today, they're used in newsletters and publications in a great many different fields (albeit in a different form than initially), where they help in marketing a wide range of products — from computers to fax machines, silica monitors to blood profile analyzers.

Where does the case history fit in the hierarchy of writing? How does it compare with the profile and the science article? A good case history describes the user, presents a concise summary of product benefits, and incorporates elements of both profile and science writing.

In much the same way as the profile tells the story of an individual, the case history relates the tale of a product and of the person who uses it. Frequently, by employing such terms as user friendly and versatile, and such descriptions as "the instrument tells us when to regenerate," the case history almost personifies the product.

The science article presents complex technical concepts in terms that the average reader can understand. The case history, on the other hand, tells how a particular person benefits from using a particular product. In a sense, the science article thus portrays a world view, while the case history presents a limited view of a specific product.

Writing successful case histories is no more or less difficult than producing profiles, or science articles, or any other form of writing — but the task is quite different. Here, then, in the following pages are some ways in which producing a case history differs from writing other forms of communication.

5.2.1 Obtain Leads for Case Histories

If you are putting together a newsletter by yourself, without anyone feeding you leads for case history articles, the daily newspaper can be one of the best sources of leads. By scanning the Business Day Section of the *New York Times*, for instance, you'll not only obtain ideas for articles but you'll be sure the information is up-to-date.

If you're writing a newsletter for a company, contact company employees for the names of satisfied users. As you might expect, company management can generally provide appropriate names for case history articles. In writing case history articles in 1990 for "news notes," a newsletter published by Scientific Instruments (Hawthorne, NY), company management supplied me with the names of five users of the company's silica monitors. Four of the five turned out to be especially helpful, and successful case history articles resulted from the interviews.

5.2.2 Obtain the Right Person's OK to Start

Be sure to obtain the right person's okay before you start your case history. This step can save a lot of time. Users generally know whose approval is needed for you to get started — but not always. It can be very frustrating when you're well along in writing a case history only to find the project suddenly vetoed by the user's supervisor, say, or by a public affairs person.

Early on, I generally ask the user in writing for an okay to write up the application: I then talk over my proposal on the telephone and, even if the user has already given his or her verbal okay, I send a letter which the user can pass along to supervision for a fully considered, official okay. A typical request is as follows:

> I have been retained by Company X to write case histories for their newsletter. In a future issue, we wish to include a write-up of your use of the Model Y analyzer. If this is satisfactory, we can set a convenient time to obtain input by telephone. I will then send you a draft of my write-up for any changes or additions you might want to make before publication.

❑ ❑ ❑

Sometimes, of course, your request will be turned down. Users employ an assortment of ways to say "No." Some users are concerned that too much of their time will be required in providing you with the necessary input; others are afraid your article may be used in promotion without their okay; still others are concerned that the article will be given or shown to others (especially their supervisors) before they've had a chance to approve it themselves.

If you receive a user's okay but still sense that he or she has reservations about your writing proposal, try to resolve such concerns before you start asking questions.

❑ ❑ ❑

If your case history is likely to be complicated, don't start asking questions during your initial conversation. Instead; set a date and time for a future interview. (This way, the user will be better prepared to answer questions.)

5.2.3 Ask User for Copies of Any Material Already Written

When the user has agreed to provide input for the case history, but before you conduct an interview, ask for copies of any information that may already be available, such as articles from the newspaper or a house organ. Helpful information sometimes shows up in unexpected places, such as the annual report or literature prepared for an open house of the facility.

5.2.4 Clear the Way for a Successful Interview

Probably the most important step in preparing for the interview is to write out your main questions in advance. Interviewing in person and interviewing by telephone both have their advantages: On-site interviewing provides opportunity to examine the product firsthand, take photographs, and hold informal discussions (such as during a break for coffee). Interviewing by telephone, on the other hand, takes less time and costs less.

If you decide to interview in person, try to do so

without a third party (a sales person, for example) being present. After all, your objectives are usually quite different from those of sales representatives or others. Your aim is to encourage the user to talk; a sales representative's objective is to make a sale. At times during the interview you may even play the devil's advocate, asking, perhaps, if the user is aware of any limitations of the product — just to start the user talking. Sales people are inclined to view such discussion as too negative.

❑ ❑ ❑

On rare occasions, others employed by the user's company — such as corporate communications personnel — insist on being present during the interview, or listening in. You have to go along in such circumstances, of course, but in general, one-to-one conversations are the most productive.

Obtaining too little input can be a problem, but getting too much input can sometimes present an even greater problem. Occasionally you may run into a user who tells you practically everything — including his company's confidential information. This can be a problem later when you have submitted a final draft for sign-off. When management reads the draft and spots the confidential information, not only will they insist that the copy be revised but they may even kill your entire write-up.

How can you prevent something like this from happening? When you first become aware that your source is telling you too much, ask whether the information should really be included in your write-up, or whether it should be considered company-confidential.

❑ ❑ ❑

Every writer is an amateur sleuth, but a writer of case histories must be a first-rate detective. To stalk a case history successfully, you will need to ask many who, what, where, when, and why questions.

At times, the user (or the user's supervisor) will turn down your proposal to write a case history on the grounds that their application is confidential. You may be able to overcome such objections, however, by assuring them that the article will not contain information of a proprietary nature.

> Editor's Note: Many writing proposals are turned down simply because the users have previously had a bad experience with other writers.

Another matter to decide before proceeding with the interview is whether to use a tape recorder. If you decide to tape-record the interview (after first obtaining the user's permission), keep in mind that even if the user says okay, the mere presence of a tape recorder can sometimes inhibit free discussion. (Taping a telephone interview, though, doesn't seem to inhibit conversation — possibly because the recording device is out of sight.)

Should a tape recorder be used? Taping the interview results in more-faithful reporting of the conversation —and is much like using shorthand.

❑ ❑ ❑

5.2.5 Leave the Door Open as to What Will Be Done with Completed Article (in Addition to Publishing in Newsletter)

Even though you may have planned initially to print the complete case history in a newsletter, you may later decide to publish only a condensation in the newsletter and submit the full write-up to a trade journal. (For this, you will first need to obtain the user's approval, of course.)

If you do intend to submit your case history to a journal, consider coauthoring with the user. Teaming up with an experienced user increases your chances of obtaining useful input when the article is being prepared, eliminates sometimes awkward direct quotations (since the user is now a coauthor), and adds credibility to the finished piece.

5.2.6 Proceed with Interview

Whether you interview in person or by telephone depends on the subject and the people involved. One important must: As the interview proceeds, if you're unsure about anything the user has said, ask for immediate clarification before continuing with the interview.

5.2.7 Identify Any Others Later Signing Off on Completed Article; Obtain Their Input

> Editor's Note: People you interview may not always be aware that others must also sign off on the completed article or that they may have important input or restrictions for it.

5.2.8 Begin Writing Immediately after Interview

Begin writing while the interview is still fresh. A case history should follow the same rules of usage and style as other forms of writing. Several points, though, are especially important when writing case histories:

(1) Describe the big picture. Even the title you assign your piece can cue readers about its breadth. A case history I once wrote about the Agricultural Laboratory

at the University of Georgia could have had the theme: How Brand X instrumentation helped the laboratory keep up to date. Instead, I decided on a broader approach and wrote about how the instruments enabled them to operate a model agricultural laboratory.

(2) Use active voice in your write-up. Vigorous, forceful words are usually more suitable for a case history than passive words. This is particularly true when the case history will appear in a newsletter where the writing is abbreviated, even staccato, in style. Subscription newsletters, for example, are usually written in active voice. Routine use of active voice results in more forceful writing and, in most instances, in shorter sentences. On both counts, reader comprehension is aided.

(3) Case histories usually contain more quotations (both direct and indirect) than other forms of writing. During the interview, try to catch the user's exact words. Later, when you're asking for approval of the completed article, you'll be more likely to get an okay if the user recognizes the words as his or her own. Of course, you'll need to correct any errors in grammar or content made by the user. For example: If the user says that use of the product eliminated the need for two laboratory technicians, write instead that it "freed up two technicians for other duties." (After all, you don't want to be even remotely connected with any elimination of technicians.)

(4) Pleasing visual arrangement of copy on the printed page of the newsletter helps get attention, but readers want good writing above everything.

If you were unable to take a photograph while

conducting the interview, ask the user to arrange for one to be taken, and offer to pay photography costs. Most users will comply readily with your request (usually by having the plant photographer or some other employee at the site take a photo), but rarely accept reimbursement.

Be sure to obtain a signed photograph release (such as the following) from each person appearing in a photograph:

> In return for consideration (copies of the case history when published) permission is hereby given to ______ to use the enclosed photograph in the newsletter, "________________."

5.2.9 When Sign-Off Is Necessary, Don't Give Out Copies of Write-Up until Final Approval Obtained

Whether or not you will need to obtain approval of your article depends on circumstances: If you're writing a long or involved case history, or if the user requires sign-off of final copy, send your completed manuscript to the user for any changes or additions — and for approval. In sending the draft to the user, you may want to leave blank spaces where further information would strengthen any parts of the article.

> Editor's Note: Users are generally quite willing to fill in blanks of a draft.

❑ ❑ ❑

Where sign-off by the user is necessary (or advisable), be sure to obtain the user's okay before giving, or even showing, a copy of the article to anyone. Some newsletters are issued so quickly, though, that there simply isn't time to request formal approval from authors before publication.

For example, take the newsletter "Control Industry Inside Report (CIIR)," published by Cahners Publishing's Control Engineering for CEOs, top marketing executives, and other subscribers. Every two weeks, Felix Tancula, editor of "CIIR," puts together another issue of this newsletter containing news about instrumentation and control.

"I assemble all copy by Tuesday of every other week — or, at the latest, by Wednesday or Thursday," says Tancula. "Newsletters are mailed the following Monday — the publication date. I cull a lot of news releases and other information in writing each issue. If I learn of some especially important development, I may phone the user (or supplier) to see if I can pick up an exclusive slant to write about. I also have a regular lineup of sources I call just to ask 'What's new?'

"After completing my write-up, I go directly into print. There isn't time to ask anyone for an okay. We're like a newspaper; we print our information now, figuring we can always issue a correction or an apology later — although I've rarely had to do so."

❑ ❑ ❑

Typically, when you send your final draft to the user, he or she will fill in blanks, make a few corrections, and return your write-up without even a cover letter. (It is recommended that you place the corrected manuscript and any photo releases in your permanent file.)

Sometimes, unfortunately, the user's management will decide that your case history contains too much product endorsement and not enough compliance with their company policy. Be patient, though! You may still obtain approval if you offer to change the copy and incorporate a disclaimer (as a footnote to, or at the beginning of, your article). In the few instances where I've used a disclaimer, I've found that a paragraph such as the following has been very effective in removing user objections:

> This article is not intended as an exclusive endorsement of Brand X computers per se, but is, rather, a description of how computer systems are used by Company Y in biological research.

5.2.10 Strive for Uniformity

Whether you're writing case histories, profiles, Q&A columns, or other kinds of articles for a newsletter, it's important to develop an editorial style that will fit both you and your audience. If more than one person is writing copy for your newsletter, strive for uniformity. One way to achieve a more consistent writing style is by issuing writing guidelines to authors, a step often taken by newsletter editors.

One publisher routinely benefiting from this practice is Simon & Schuster's Bureau of Business Practice (BBP) (Waterford, CT), who publish a variety of newsletters. One BBP newsletter, the twice-monthly "Construction Supervision & Safety Letter," provides information on increasing the effectiveness of supervisors of blue-collar workers by maintaining a safe worksite. The editor of this BBP newsletter provides "Writer's Guidelines" to all would-be authors contributing to the newsletter.

The effectiveness of guidelines for writers at BBP is shown by examining an article on forklift safety in the December 15, 1990, issue of "Construction Supervision & Safety Letter." The thrust of this article is that a forklift is a potentially dangerous machine, but a good forklift safety training program can prevent accidents.

TABLE 5-1 Comparison of writer's guidelines and finished article on forklift safety at Simon & Schuster's Bureau of Business Practice.

BBP's Writer's Guidelines	Finished Article on Forklift Safety
"Most articles run 400-750 words. If you exceed this, don't worry — we usually tighten up material."	The forklift article has 1100 words. (Enough for tightening up.)
"A story should contain three essentials: (1) A problem (2) A solution (3) A benefit	The article gives a succinct statement of the problem; it cites National Safety Council statistics to back up the statement that a forklift is a potentially dangerous machine: "Forklift accidents caused more than 34,000 medical emergencies in 1987."
"Many of our readers have come up through the ranks. ...They're interested in goals."	The article states: "A good forklift safety training program can prevent accidents ..."
"Give [supervisors] practical how-to tips they can use with their own crews."	The article presents a practical, comprehensive operator training program, including a checklist of 20 specific safety rules.

A comparison of BBP guidelines and finished article (TABLE 5-1) shows that the author has indeed followed the guidelines. (Copyrighted material reprinted with permission of CONSTRUCTION AND SAFETY LETTER and Bureau of Business Practice, 24 Rope Ferry Road, Waterford, CT 06386.)

❑ ❑ ❑

Most people starting a newsletter select sources of information and a field of inquiry or subject with which they are familiar. Roy Roecker did even better: he started a newsletter-publishing business in the very field in which he had worked as an employee of General Electric Company.

In 1974, Roecker was an employee of General Electric R&D in Schenectady, NY, where he was responsible for gathering information and issuing it to the various GE facilities. After four years, GE discontinued this endeavor and gave Roecker approval to start his own business of marketing the same information. Except for an interval during which Roecker sold his business, then bought it back again, he has been publishing newsletters ever since. As Prestwick Publishing, Inc., Roecker now publishes four different newsletters: "New from Japan," "New from Europe," "New from U.S.", and "Electronics from the World."

❑ ❑ ❑

You may want to include a column in your newsletter—perhaps bylined by you, an associate, or someone well known in the field. The "Printing Association of Florida Newsletter" frequently contains the column, "Q&A: Dear Marion", written by Marion Clark, president of Unemployment Services, Inc., a private company which helps Florida employers fight improper unemployment claims and reduce unemployment taxes. The column discusses such matters as the impact of legislation on industry.

❑ ❑ ❑

Q&A columns work well in newsletters; they are particularly effective in newsletters dealing with complex subjects. The reason? Questions can be used to break up long sections of complicated copy. Consider the newsletter "Science Watch," published by ISI Institute for Scientific Information (Philadelphia, PA):

> "Our newsletter tracks trends and performance in basic research, monitoring about 3,200 scientific journals published around the world," says David A. Pendlebury, editor. The newsletter, which is published ten times a year, uses an 8 1/2 by 11, 8-page format and contains a Q&A column in each issue. Over a third of the newsletter's November 1990 issue, for example, is devoted to a Q&A article — admittedly quite technical — about the new trans-Pacific fiber-optic communications line scheduled to be laid by 1996.

Based on an interview with Professor Emmanuel Desurvire of Columbia University, the article deals with amplifiers made of the element erbium. Questions addressed to Professor Desurvire include the following:

> What are the amplifier's chief uses? Its advantages? Will quality improve? What about the related area of erbium fiber lasers? Is additional research now underway?

In effect, the interviewer uses the traditional who,

what, when type of questions to break up a complex body of copy. The result: a successful Q&A article.

❑ ❑ ❑

Advances in research and development provide a useful source of information for newsletters. In the July/August 1991 issue of "SB News," published by SmithKline Beecham (SB) (Philadelphia, PA), for example, a major issue is examined. Dr. George Poste, chairman of R&D for SB, discusses the company's research and development organization. Poste presents his views on the changes facing the pharmaceutical industry and stresses the importance of adapting to these changes.

"I and my colleagues," says Poste, "are responsible for interpreting the factors that are causing science to move ever faster — causing change in the pharmaceutical business. The people who report to me must explain to their groups what it means, specifically, to them. Communication has never been more important."

❑ ❑ ❑

If, while putting together an issue of your newsletter, you find that you're a little short of copy, you may find it helpful to use one or more fillers. These brief pieces can be obtained from any of several sources, such as the newsletter "Fillers for Publications," published by Fillers for Publications (Albuquerque, NM).

"We provide fillers that can be used as is," says Pat Johnston, manager of "Fillers for Publications," "or writers can reset them to their own type specifications." The basic fillers — eight pages in length — consist of tips on health and exercise, highlights of scientific developments, historical briefs, anecdotes, and a variety of other items. One filler, for example, consists of 15 lines about John Campbell, who "published the first edition of the 'Boston News-Letter' in 1704."

A "Brainstorming" section on the back page of "Fillers for Publications" gives writers suggestions on composing headlines and page 5 provides "Comprehensive Column Stretchers." These stretchers, each two or three lines in length by 14 picas wide, are offered for filling out a column that's too short. The stretchers are generally philosophical or social commentaries — some humorous, some serious — composed by well-known writers or by staff members of "Fillers for Publications."

"We market fillers for every conceivable industry or service," says Johnston. "That's why our fillers deal with such a wide range of topics."

❑ ❑ ❑

5.2.11 Publish Telephone Numbers for Ordering, Requesting Service, and Obtaining Further Information

A different kind of "filler" than those mentioned in the preceding section consists of a list of telephone numbers — such as phone numbers for placing orders — printed for the convenience of readers.

5.2.12 Consider Publishing Reprints of Technical Papers

At times you may want to send a particular technical paper to your readers, but the paper may be too long to print in your newsletter. Even if divided into several parts and printed in installments, this would still be impractical. One solution to this dilemma is to print an abstract of the paper in the newsletter and offer copies of the full paper by reply card. (If many papers are to be handled in this manner, be sure to assign code numbers to the various papers to keep track of who is requesting what.)

5.2.13 Solicit Contributions from Readers or Experts in the Field

Bylined articles — solicited as well as contributed — are an important source of information for newsletters. Articles may be written by either inside or outside authors; some outside authors are paid, some are not. Articles for newsletters published by The Cobb Group (Louisville, KY) illustrate the different possible arrangements. The Cobb Group has been publishing newsletters since 1984, when the company launched its first newsletter. Just recently, the company introduced five additional newsletters, bringing their total to more than 30.

"Most of our newsletters use a combination of solicited and contributed articles," says Cobb Group's Kathleen Lane. "In addition, users send us ideas for articles. Although we don't consider these voluntary suggestions as useful as contributed articles, we do give these people a fee for their ideas."

Authors of articles for Cobb Group newsletters write copy in Word, which is then switched by the Production Department to PageMaker on a Macintosh, and finally printed. Mostly, Cobb newsletters use in-house authors, and they try to write all newsletters in the same style. Cobb Group uses some outside authors for newsletters such as The DOS Authority and Inside Turbo C++. Sign-off of completed articles is required by three groups: authors, editors, and production people.

❑ ❑ ❑

Readers are generally quite willing to write articles for publication in newsletters. Take book reviews, for instance. Book reviews in newsletters are like reviews in magazines and other publications — with one exception: book reviews in newsletters can be more precisely targeted to meet the specific interests and needs of readers.

Book reviews are published frequently in "Computer Communication Review," a quarterly newsletter of the ACM Special Interest Group on Data Communication. The book, "The Art of Computer Systems Performance Analysis: Techniques for Experimental Design, Measurement, Simulation, and Modelling," by Raj Jain (John Wiley and Sons, 1991) was reviewed in the newsletter's January 1991 issue. Both the choice of which book to review and the emphasis of the review itself are right on target for this newsletter's readers.

The ACM reviewer, Craig Partridge, opens by saying that the goal of the book is to "comprehensively survey the field of computer performance analysis." He then proceeds to tell how well the author meets this goal. The reviewer closes by saying that the text is "a pleasure to read, a surprise for a highly mathematical book. Furthermore, the frequent use of case studies was effective and sometimes entertaining."

A guest column or guest editorial in your newsletter can sometimes be an effective way to communicate with readers, particularly if you're putting together a newsletter issue for a large marketing organization. Written by qualified outside persons, guest columns allow a different perspective to be presented on some topic covered in the newsletter. Likely candidates for writing such a column include members of trade associations, educators, consulting engineers, and spokespersons for governmental regulatory agencies (such as the FDA or the EPA). Q&A formats usually work well for this purpose.

> Editor's Note: You won't be able to change what your outside author says in the column, of course, but you can add an introductory paragraph or two. For example, you may want to explain how the author is especially well qualified to write on the subject.

❑ ❑ ❑

Most newsletters encourage readers to write to the editor if they have a problem or want to communicate with other readers. "The Portable Paper," for example, publishes letters to the editor containing tips for operating Hewlett-Packard's portable products.

❑ ❑ ❑

Another publisher using both solicited and contributed articles is Information Intelligence Inc. (III), (Phoenix, AZ). At III, articles are sometimes solicited for two newsletters, "Online Newsletter" and "Online Libraries and Microcomputers."

The first of these, "Online Newsletter," is international in scope and covers online and CD-ROM developments throughout the world. "Online Libraries and Microcomputers," in contrast, is aimed at library and information center developments and applications throughout North America.

"In addition to soliciting articles from authors who are recognized experts in the field," says Richard

Huleatt, president & publisher of III, "we also receive contributed articles. We edit all articles received, but if there's a possibility that our editing may have changed the meaning of an article — or even the intent of a sentence — copy is returned to the author for approval. We correct copy for grammar and spelling, but anything further would be an editorial no-no.

"Just a few of us work on the newsletters. In addition to the authors, the staff consists of George Machovec, editor of 'Online Libraries and Microcomputers,' and myself. Fortunately, we both write in much the same style." (When their writing was analyzed recently with a software program, Corporate Voice, their writing styles were found to be within 87 percent of agreement.)

"Most formatting and other work on the III newsletters is done automatically on the computers themselves," says Huleatt. "Ever since we began in 1980, we've believed in full automation. Starting with Apple II computers, we worked our way around to IBM equipment.

"We often use our own databases to see what we ourselves may have written on a particular subject in the past. Or we may go up on several databases to doublecheck references, or to see whether anyone has covered the same ground before. We certainly don't want to come out with a feature article if someone has written on that very topic before.

"We only publish about 10 percent of the material we receive. Much of the remaining copy is what we refer to as 'vaporware,' since it evaporates when we try to nail it down. For example: A representative of a software company says they're about to introduce a new software product ... but it never happens!"

5.2.14 Encourage Reader Contributions by Offering Compensation, Such as Book, Software, or Subscription

5.2.15 Obtain Approval from Others Before Using Their Copy ... And Always Credit the Source.

5.2.16 In Writing Case Histories, Consider Using Quotation Marks

Direct quotations carry more weight than indirect quotations. Be careful, though, not to have too many direct quotes in your copy.

5.2.17 If You Also Plan to Submit Newsletter Articles to a Journal, Check Its Policy on Quotes

Some trade journals request authors not to use direct quotes at all, so it pays to check before submitting a manuscript.

5.2.18 References

The addition of references, or a bibliography, to an article substantiates the article and increases its credibility and usefulness. In fact, the inclusion of references and footnotes constitutes one of the differences between newsletter articles and papers in journals: Newsletter articles rarely contain references; journal papers must use them.

One newsletter that uses references at times is "The Latham Letter," published by The Latham Foundation (Alameda, CA). "The Latham Letter," which typically runs 24 pages in length, is a special-interest-group newsletter. It publishes articles on such topics as human/companion animal bonds, pet-facilitated therapy, ecology, and humane education ... as well as articles describing the goals and accomplishments of The Latham Foundation.

"'The Latham Letter' has become a resource for students and practitioners alike," says Madeleine C. Pitts, its editor. "It is cited frequently in research work."

> Editor's Note: The use of references at the end of a newsletter article makes it more useful and enhances the reader's regard for the article — and for the newsletter.

5.2.19 Trade Shows

Information about trade shows can be readily communicated via newsletter. Occasionally, the organization that sponsors a trade show also issues a newsletter with information about the show. The Printing Association of Florida, Inc., for example, sponsors the newsletter "Printing Association of Florida Newsletter." It also holds the "Graphics of the Americas" show each year, a large show with exhibitors from all over the U.S. In 1991, "Graphics of the Americas" attracted 18,000 persons (over a three-day period) to its sixteenth show in Miami.

CHAPTER SIX

Newsletter Start-Up

Getting a 4-Page Newsletter Off the Ground

To launch a newsletter successfully takes thorough planning and a good understanding of the basic steps involved. Experience in starting up newsletters has shown that actual costs for the first year can average one-and-a-half to two times the amount originally estimated, according to newsletter specialists.

Specific steps for designing a newsletter are given in this chapter. In addition to planning the design of the newsletter, however, it's also important that you consider its distribution. To accomplish this, it's recommended that you visit your local post office early in your planning and talk over your distribution plans. (If your newsletters will be mailed first class, speak with the information clerk. If they will be mailed third class, talk with the person in charge of bulk mailings.)

While at the post office, ask to see a copy of the *Domestic Mail Manual*, a publication containing over 900 pages of detailed postal regulations. After your newsletter project has moved further along, you may want to subscribe to this publication. Information on subscribing can be obtained from the Superintendent of Documents, U.S. Government Printing Office: telephone (202) 512-2303. Or, you can order a one-year susbscription by using the order form in the manual.

6.1 Corporate Newsletter Start-Up

Assume, for example, that you're putting together a four-page corporate newsletter for a manufacturer of computers. The various steps in starting up such a newsletter are as follows:

Step 1) In conjunction with your client — the computer manufacturer — establish design specifications for the newsletter. (Typical design specs are shown in TABLE 6-1).

Step 2) Plan contents for the first issue. Strive for balance; assume the newsletter will contain the following five articles: (Refer to preliminary layout in FIGURE 6-1)

a. Introduction

b. Feature Article: Q&A interview of company president

c. Application Corner: New software available

d. Maintenance Tips: Troubleshooting the computer

e. Secondary Article: Some recent computer advances

Step 3) Decide whether the newsletter will be typeset, produced by desktop publishing, photocopied from the output of a word processor, or reproduced in some other manner. (Assume, for this example, that galleys will be typeset.) Obtain a cost estimate on the

TABLE 6-1 Design specifications for 4-page corporate newsletter

Size: Four pages, each 8 1/2 by 11 inches
Paper: One 11 by 17 inch sheet, folded in half; 70 to 80 pound coated stock
Headlines: 20 point Palatino
Subheads: 12 point Palatino
Body Copy: 10 point Helvetica; three columns per page; columns on pages 2, 3, and 4 to be 9 inches in depth; columns on page 1 to be 7 inches in depth (depending on the size of the masthead); 1-pica gutters; approximately 7 lines of copy per column-inch; each column to be 14 picas (approximately 36 characters and spaces) in width.
Captions: 9 point Bold Helvetica
Side Margins: 5/8 inches wide (for later 3-hole punching.)
Footer: Company logo, 9 point Bold Palatino, all caps
Masthead: "Computer Notes," 72 point Bold Helvetica

following basis from a typesetter having full graphic capabilities:

- Quantities to be produced: 3,000 newsletters and 1,000 reply cards. The newsletters will be printed with black ink and a second color (process blue) on pages 1 and 4. Also, assume the newsletters will not be 3-hole punched, but will be folded (for mailing) to 3 3/4 by 8 1/2 inches in size. Folded newsletters will be sealed with a small piece of transparent tape.

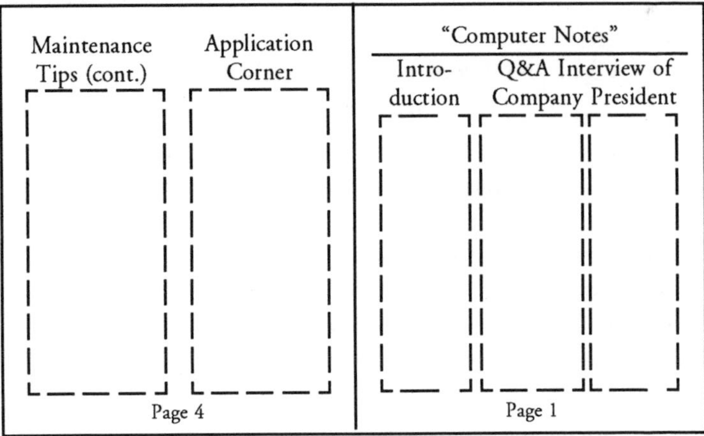

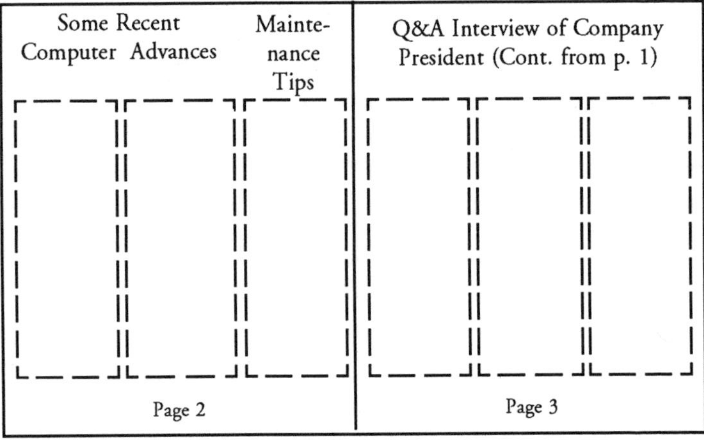

Figure 6-1: Preliminary layout of corporate newsletter

- Reply cards will be 3 3/4 by 6 inches, printed on card stock.(Questionnaire on one side of card; franked [postage paid] return address of client on the back. Reply cards to be inserted in folded newsletters.)

Step 4) Provide the typesetter you have selected with a few representative pages of your document, and request that this sample be set in type in accordance with the specifications in TABLE 6-1. Then adjust the information in TABLE 6-1 so that it is in agreement with the sample data.

Step 5) Obtain approval of both your copy and the cost estimate from the computer manufacturer you're writing for ... having previously obtained a sign-off of copy from any outside company you're writing about.

Step 6) Determine the average number of characters and spaces per line of input copy in your manuscript, regardless of whether this copy has been printed out by computer, typwritten, or written by hand. (Assume, for this example, that this count is 72, a common count for typewritten manuscripts). Knowing, from TABLE 6-1, that each line of the basic design contains 36 characters and spaces (depending, of course, on how the manuscript is laid out), note that each line of input copy will fill two lines (72/36) of the printed newsletter.

Step 7) Without taking headlines or captions into consideration for this first approximation, make a quick check to see if you have the proper amount of copy.

Step 8) Note (from FIGURE 6-1) that the printed newsletter will consist of 9 columns (each 9 inches deep) on pages 2, 3, and 4, plus 3 columns on the front page (each 7 inches deep). This totals 102 column-inches for the four pages of the newsletter. At approximately 7 lines per inch (TABLE 6-1), the printed newsletter will contain a total of 714 lines.

Step 9) If, for example, your input copy contains 25 lines per page, you will need a little over 14 pages [714/(25 X 2)] of input manuscript to fill the issue.

Step 10) As a more rigorous check, go through the calculations again, this time allowing for headlines, figures, captions, sub-heads, etc., which can reduce the line-count appreciably. If you find that you need additional copy (or have too much), take steps to adjust the amount of copy accordingly.

Step 11) Obtain galleys from printer, and proofread the copy.

Step 12) Prepare a rough writer's visual, with photocopies of the galleys stripped in position. Obtain corrected galleys from the printer for any corrections needed. (You don't need to proofread all of the corrected galleys —just the paragraphs where you've made changes.)

> Editor's Note: Remember, you don't pay for any typos made by the typesetter. You do pay for author's alterations, however. (Even minor alterations can cause the typesetter to shift copy or readjust the fit.)

Step 13) Obtain final approval of writer's visual; proceed with printing of the newsletter.

> Editor's Note: The specifications presented in this example are typical of those used in producing a

four-page newsletter. Information on these specs was provided by Ace Graphics Inc., a center for graphic arts services, located in Tenafly, NJ.

6.2 Individual or Entrepreneurial Newsletter Start-Up

If you're starting up a newsletter by yourself—as an entrepreneur or otherwise—start-up will be both simpler and more complicated than if you are part of a corporate launch team. On the one hand, you can make decisions without waiting for others to concur. On the other hand, you will have only yourself to blame if your decisions go awry.

6.3 Some DOs and DON'Ts for Putting Together a Newsletter

On interviewing:

When interviewing someone for an article in your newsletter, always be ready to jot down (or tape-record) what is being said. This doesn't mean just during the interview itself but all the time. Whether you're touring the site, say, or having lunch with the interviewee, keep in mind that spur-of-the-moment input under relaxed and informal conditions can sometimes be the most useful of all information.

❑ ❑ ❑

On getting the reader's attention:

Readers only look at pages that catch their attention. If a drawing looks uninteresting, for example, the reader may simply skip to another article. By including a gray (10-15 percent) screen, however, you can make a complex drawing more interesting. Remember, after content, readers rate appearance next in importance.

❑ ❑ ❑

If you want to add a second color to your 4-page newsletter, but your budget won't stand the expense, consider adding the second color to just the front and back pages.

❑ ❑ ❑

If a particular newsletter article has both a headline and, on the same page, one or more subheads, it's generally recommended that the type used for the headline be at least two sizes larger than the type used for the subhead(s).

❑ ❑ ❑

To emphasize points in an article, consider copying one or two key sentences from the article and highlighting them. (Such visual treatment is expandable and makes a good filler.) Thus:

Copy One or Two Key Sentences from Article; Emphasize in Some Manner

❑ ❑ ❑

Don't make the columns of your newsletter too wide. Readers generally feel most comfortable with columns that are about 1 1/2 alphabets (characters and spaces) wide.

❑ ❑ ❑

Don't use oversize type for your headlines; type that's too large is ponderous and ungainly.

❑ ❑ ❑

If your newsletter contains copy by an outside author, and the newsletter is free (or very reasonable) in price, don't forget to send a complimentary copy or two to the author.

❑ ❑ ❑

On preparing copy:

When writing a newsletter article about a product, it's better to emphasize the benefits of the product than to attack competition by name.

❑ ❑ ❑

If an article is very long, make it easy on your readers by placing an italicized summary at the beginning of the article — or in a separate box.

❑ ❑ ❑

Divide up exceptionally long articles. An article that's especially long can be divided into Parts I and II and published in separate issues of your newsletter ... or you can publish a condensation in the newsletter and offer the entire article to readers requesting it via reply card.

❑ ❑ ❑

Don't print future dates if they're likely to have passed by the time the newsletter is printed. Instead, list *scheduled* events rather than *coming* events.

❑ ❑ ❑

Regardless of whether your newsletters are sold or

distributed at no charge, you can gain readers and/or income by publishing a list of back issues and topics.

❑ ❑ ❑

If an article for your newsletter needs clarification, place a paragraph or two of explanation at the beginning of the article. It saves you the inconvenience of asking the author to revise the article.

❑ ❑ ❑

On signing off:

Remember, a sign-off isn't just for approval; it also tells you whether you have your facts straight.

CHAPTER SEVEN

Increase Newsletter Effectiveness

Start by Examining Track Records

The first step recommended for improving an established newsletter is to examine the track records of successful newsletters. After that, steps for increasing newsletter effectiveness include the following:

- Examine "how to" books containing information on newsletters; a variety of such books can be found at bookstores and at most large libraries.
- Send out one or two samples of your newsletter to each of your prospects.
- Ask some of your readers for suggestions as to how your newsletter can be improved.

7.1 Newsletter Associations Lead The Way

You can obtain useful information on launching

newsletters from a number of trade associations, including the following:

7.1.1 The Newsletter Publisher's Association (NPA)

The mission of the Newsletter Publisher's Association (NPA) is "to represent the interests of, and provide information to, publishers of for-profit newsletters and specialized information services." The NPA represents "nearly 700 publishers producing over 2,000 newsletters and other information services."

7.2 Newsletter Directories Point The Direction

Newsletter directories not only provide basic information about specific newsletters, but they usually contain an overview of newsletters in general.

7.2.1 Fourth (1990) Edition of the Serials Directory

This directory lists over 140 major subject headings (plus another 133 sub-headings) of publications; newsletters are published in approximately 80-percent of these categories.

7.2.2 Oxbridge Directory of Newsletters

The Oxbridge Directory of Newsletters: 1991 is published by Oxbridge Communications, Inc. (NY, NY). Its ninth edition lists over 21,000 newsletters.

7.2.3 Newsletters in Print

Newsletters in Print (NIP), edited by Robert J. Huffman and John Krol, provides information on more than 10,000 newsletters and other publications available in print or online. Formerly known as *Newsletters Directory,* the Fifth Edition (1991-92) of NIP is a descriptive guide to newsletters of various types. Newsletters on local politics, community organizations, and the like, are not included.

7.2.4 Newsnet

Newsnet, a service of Dun & Bradstreet, Inc. (Bryn Mawr, PA), is a current-awareness database of online business information and intelligence. Newsnet offers a wide range of business information; for example, more than 500 newsletters are available in full text. And, because information about newsletters is supplied directly to Newsnet, it can be accessed immediately — usually before it's even in print.

7.3 Key Newsletters Targeted at Various Audiences

7.3.1 Hotline

The "Hotline" is published by the Newsletter Publisher's Association (NPA). A members-only publication, the "Hotline" is published 24 times a year.

7.4 Newsletters Used to Advantage

Among the people who benefit most from publishing their own newsletters are professionals in the business of supplying information. Such people include editors, writers, lawyers, doctors, consultants, designers, accountants, and public relations people.

Since newsletters are such an effective means of communication, they provide many benefits to those who publish them. For example, for almost a decade, Louis Slesin has published his newsletter "Microwave

News," with information about how electromagnetism has adverse health effects (il por Time, 136:53 Jl 30 '90). Slesin's basic message is that radiation, emitted from power lines, computer terminals, and other technologies may present a definite health hazard. Although the circulation of his newsletter (according to our latest information) is just over 500 copies, Slesin and his newsletter have become well known in scientific and professional circles and he is in a position to influence readers.

❑ ❑ ❑

Another newsletter with a specific objective — cutting down on waste — is "Government Waste-Watch," published by Citizens Against Government Waste (CAGW) (Washington, DC). CAGW is a nonpartison, nonprofit educational organization, and its newsletter is issued quartlerly. "Government Waste-Watch" publishes articles dealing with such subjects as wasteful legislation, alleged overcharging of the government, new taxes, and increased government. Bylined articles typically describe how a $5 million boondoggle was slipped into a multimillion dollar spending bill; how waste is being ignored; and what reforms could be adopted by Congress to curb waste, fraud, and abuse.

❑ ❑ ❑

Members of Congress are well aware of the benefits of communicating with constituents on a regular basis. Most Congressional offices, in fact, issue a newsletter more or less regularly. U.S. Representative Gerry E. Studds, Democrat from Massachusetts, for example, regularly issues "The Weekly Report to the People."

Public utilities find newsletters especially useful for PR purposes and for providing customers with useful information. Look, for example, at "OR ServiceLine," published by Orange and Rockland Utilities, Inc. (Pearl River, NY). The newsletter's Spring 1991 issue included the following "how to" information:

- How O&R customers experiencing financial hardship can apply to The Neighbor Fund for help. (The Fund is administered by the Salvation Army.)
- How customer families whose primary wage earners have been called to active military duty can apply to The Neighbor Fund for assistance.
- How customers can protect sensitive electronic equipment from momentary power interruptions.
- How customers can determine which service lines and wiring are their own responsibility and which are O&R's.
- Where customers can write for information on eligibility for lower Time-of-Use (TOU) rates.
- How O&R's recently initiated recycling program is demonstrating that the company is a good environmental citizen.

❑ ❑ ❑

Large clubs also distribute newsletters. Club newsletters keep members informed of coming events, give them a sense of belonging (an important objective), and reassure them that their membership is indeed something of value.

❑ ❑ ❑

Newsletters are particularly well suited for dissemination of information about coming events, since newsletters can be readily published or revised at the last minute. For example, the "Printing Association of Florida Newsletter" encourages attendance at the annual Graphics of the Americas show.

It's often said (but is probably worth repeating) that no matter what the subject, there is probably a newsletter being published somewhere today that deals with that very topic. For example, "International Living," edited by Kathleen Peddicord, Baltimore, MD, specializes in profiles of famous and infamous Americans living abroad. Another example is "Today's Parts Manager," published by Management Computer Systems (Columbus, OH). This newsletter, which has only recently started up, publishes information on management topics of possible interest to General Motors parts managers.

Looking for a newsletter on travel? "Sailaway," a six-page newsletter issued by Travel Agents International (St. Petersburg, FL), may be just the answer, since it deals exclusively with cruise travel. Closer to home, the quarterly newsletter "Nursing Mom," edited by Jeanie Donaldson (Inyokern, CA), deals with breast-feeding mothers.

❑ ❑ ❑

Some newsletters tell readers flat out how their information can be used to advantage; others use a "soft sell" approach.

7.4.1 To Make a Profit

Of all the companies that both market a product and publish a newsletter, it's reported less than a third know how much, or whether, the newsletter affects their business.

Newsletter publishers are always anxious to know the chances of their newsletters surviving. But such survival information is generally held confidential; most newsletter publishers reveal very little about their revenues. Survival information on magazines, by contrast, is more readily available for analysis. In October 1991 *The New York Times*, for example, reported on a magazine survival study at the Magazine Service Journalism Program at the University of Mississippi. According to the *Times*, 1238 new magazines were started during the years 1985-1989. Of these, a surprising 35.5 percent (almost double the survival rate for magazines started in the period 1981-1983) were still being published.

> Editor's Note: Although most associations and individual companies in the newsletter field have statistics on newsletter survival, their information is generally not accessible to the public.

7.4.2 To Meet Other Objectives

The newsletter is a unique communications tool capable of reaching readers with just about any message the writer or publisher wants readers to receive.

Consider survey results, for example, which are often reported by newsletters. "Securities Week" (a newsletter no longer being published) reported (in its 12-page issue of March 18, 1991) the results of the semiannual "Securities Week" research survey of 40 firms. One of its findings: the number of research personnel on Wall Street dropped in the second half of 1990, as many companies, particularly the larger firms and wire houses, pared back in response to market conditions.

❑ ❑ ❑

Somewhere, there is probably a newsletter that targets just about any group you can name. For example, the newsletter "View" (Snowmass Village, CO) is published mainly for the purpose of communicating with its students.

❑ ❑ ❑

CHAPTER EIGHT

Circulation

Lifeblood of the Newsletter

8.1 Build Your Newsletter Circulation

Newsletters, used in conjunction with reply cards, can help build your mailing list. In fact, a variety of innovative ways are used by newsletter publishers to increase circulation. One approach involves the use of reply cards mailed out by an affiliated publication. Take the "Cooper-Hewitt Newsletter," for instance. This membership newsletter is published by the Cooper-Hewitt National Museum of Design, an arm of the Smithsonian Institution (Washington, DC). Reply cards in the *Smithsonian*, the monthly magazine for Smithsonian members, invite readers to become members of the Cooper-Hewitt also. By becoming members of the Museum of Design, they automatically receive copies of the "Cooper-Hewitt Newsletter," among other benefits.

8.2 Keep Mailing List Up to Date

Keeping your mailing list up to date is every bit as important as building a list in the first place. The following is one effective way to update your list of names. Insert a brief paragraph or two in your newsletter explaining that the list is being brought up to date, and include instructions for filling out the reply card. If your computer system includes a database program, it can probably be used to help you compute subscription statistics, send out order acknowledgments, calculate sales taxes, and track expiration dates and subscription terms.

There are several types of mailing lists: your own in-house list, a direct-mail response list, leased lists, and miscellaneous lists such as a list of attendees at a trade show. Also available are database programs that can handle mailing list maintenance; these programs can be obtained from such sources as IBM PC and Macintosh.

❑ ❑ ❑

To help you build and update your mailing list, a number of companies offer CD-ROM products. For example, one company —Phone Disc USA Corp. of Marblehead, MA — has been marketing a national directory on CD-ROM since 1990. "Phone Disc" consists of two disks covering the entire U.S.: some 90 million names. With the CD-ROM directory, a newsletter staffer responsible for circulation can use a PC to obtain the phone number and address of virtually anyone in the U.S. (This may be the solution to mailing lists that have out-of-date or incomplete listings.)

❑ ❑ ❑

Advances in on-line database and CD-ROM technologies are being made with increasing frequency, and publishers report advantages in using these technologies to build newsletter circulation. For example, Trinet America, Inc., (Parsippany, NJ) and its parent American Business Information, Inc., (Omaha, NB) market "Business Lists-on-Disk" containing information on over nine million businesses. Using "Business Lists-on-Disk," you can call up such information as name and address, a description of the business, number of employees, and names of key purchasing executives.

For over five years now, government, businesses, and the larger publishers have used CD-ROM to store important information. During this period there have been many advances in the CD-ROM technology. In May 1991, for example, The Sony Corporation introduced a product that is expected to result in increased use of CD-ROM by small companies and consumers. The Sony product, known as a Laser Library, is reported to be an offshoot of the compact disk machine. It is connected to a PC, where a single disk can store up to 250,000 pages of text.

> Editor's Note: By 1995, expect that on-line and CD-ROM services will enable you to build and update mailing lists even more efficiently than today.

❑ ❑ ❑

To cull inactive names from your mailing list and update addresses, the post office offers two services:

- You can print the words "Address Correction Requested" on your mailing piece. If the name or address is incorrect, your piece will be returned to you with the corrected address or the reason for non-delivery. There is a 35 cent charge for this service.

- Alternatively, you can print "Forwarding and Address Correction Requested" on your mailing piece. In this case, your piece will be forwarded to the corrected address (rather than being returned to you) and you will be notified of the change. For this service, you will be charged 35 cents (for first class mail up to one ounce), and the addressee will be requested to pay 29 cents (if the piece is accepted). Note: the above charges are correct as of September 15, 1992.

CHAPTER NINE

Improve Newsletter Uniformity with a Stylebook

Readers Deserve It

Many newsletters use stylebooks, or style manuals, in one form or another. Indeed, almost a quarter of all newsletter editors and writers use stylebooks to help them establish uniformity, say communicators. These style guides vary from the simple spelling directories found in most personal computers ... to extensive manuals such as the well-known *Chicago Manual of Style* and *McGraw-Hill Style Manual*.

Actually, style guides are published by many different sources, from book publishing houses and technical societies to law review associations and magazine publishers. Published primarily for the use of their own editors and writers, style guides can be obtained from libraries and bookstores as well as the publishers themselves.

Consistent communication has always been important, but consistency is especially important today. People have less time for reading these days, and when they do read, they want well-organized, consistent material. Today's readers want publications that tell them precisely what they want to know, without wasting time. This is where the stylebook comes in. It provides a means of achieving direct, up-to-date copy with emphasis on uniformity.

If you're preparing to launch a newsletter, you may want a convenient way to make sure that all terms are used consistently. Or you may be looking for a way to standardize such things as abbreviations and acronyms. Or perhaps you want to make sure that outside writers will follow your writing style. If so, you can benefit from the use of a style guide; it serves as a reference on punctuation, abbreviations, margins and spacing, trademarks, logos, and a wide range of other parameters of the printed page.

- Editor's Note: Decide what portions of a style guide you want to follow (or prepare a guide of your own). Install this on your computer system or use it manually.

❑ ❑ ❑

This is not to suggest that two writers' copy should read exactly the same. In fact, just the opposite! An invention that may reduce writers' appropriation of other writers' copy was reported in *The New York Times* on January 7, 1992. A "plagiarism machine" invented by Walter Stewart and Dr. Ned Feder scans two or more documents and boldfaces the text whenever 30 or more characters are identical.

❑ ❑ ❑

Style guides are used routinely by many publications. One newsletter using a style guide regularly is the "Apple Library Users Group (ALUG) Newsletter." Published quarterly by Apple Computer, Inc., "ALUG" provides information for users of Apple computers in libraries and information centers.

"In producing this newsletter," says Monica Ertel, editor of *"ALUG,"* "a style guide is used for such things as proper placement of the dash and how to handle illustrations." For convenience, the style guide has been loaded on a desktop publishing system comprised of a Macintosh ii, PageMaker 4.0, and LaserWriter MTX.

"ALUG" receives many contributed articles, which vary from one to five pages in length and are usually submitted by librarians. "Rarely do we find it necessary to request articles," says Ertel. "Contributed material just keeps coming in."

After receiving an article, the first step is to edit it. The "ALUG" staff tries not to alter individual writing styles of the various contributors. Sometimes, however, the process of editing causes a change in context, says Ertel. In such instances the articles are sent back to the originators for rewriting.

Although "ALUG" does not make cash payments, contributors reviewing a book or writing about a piece of software, for example, are generally given the book or software.

❑ ❑ ❑

At the Library of Michigan (Lansing, MI), style guides are created for each of 900 annual publications and stored electronically. "It's important to be able to call up the formatting used on previous issues, says John Rummel, public information officer. With everything preformatted, they simply "click to load the appropriate style guide from a file server and begin typing the new issue without having to set any parameters." If, for example, they want to work on "Access," the Library's newsletter for librarians, it's only necessary to find the "Access" master stylesheet on the menu and click it. The system then automatically loads the proper program (e.g., PageMaker) required to run it.

Warren Publishing Inc., also uses a stylebook; consistent abbreviations in 12 of Warren Publishing's newsletters, for example, are routinely established by use of a style guide. "Also," says Paul Warren, senior editor, "we have special acronyms that we use on first reference. In addition, we routinely omit the use of articles (*a*, *an*, and *the*) in all copy."

9.1 Set Standards for Layout, Spacing, Hyphenation, Pagination, etc.

Refer to CHAPTER SIX.

9.2 Use Trademarks Properly

A style guide can help you make proper use of trademarks belonging to the company for whom you're writing. If many trademarks are involved, save a list of trademarks on your computer, together with their generics, for quick reference.

CHAPTER TEN

Word Processing and Desktop Publishing

From Software to Hardware

Newsletters can be written and edited more efficiently today through the use of state-of-the-art word processing and desktop publishing (DTP). It's not possible to talk about word processing without reference to desktop publishing; the two technologies are interrelated, and are continually changing and being improved.

Just a few years ago, word processors were used to generate documents for DTP. Today, word processors in combination with laser printers are capable of producing high quality copy. Word processors such as WordPerfect, WordStar, Lotus Manuscript, and Express Publisher, for example, offer quality that comes very close to DTP and typesetting.

DTP — the ability to print your newsletter (or other document) while at your desk — is fast becoming the printing method of choice in many companies and institutions. In schools, where it is known as *classroom publishing*, desktop publishing is now used much more widely. Probably the main benefit of desktop publishing is its ability to simplify graphic arts and design. With DTP, newsletter publishers have access to a variety of software packages that are simpler to use.

Using desktop publishing, one person can perform a wide range of publishing tasks, from word processing and editing...to creating illustrations, composing pages, and printing camera-ready pages on a laser printer.

Without word processors, though, DTP would not be as cost-effective as it is. For example, the text of a 200-page research report can be readily generated using a simple word processor such as Professional Write, and the computer then switched to a program having graphics capability, such as PageMaker. In some instances, it may be necessary to switch first to an intermediate program (Professional Write to Microsoft Word to PageMaker) but this additional step usually takes only minutes.

DTP involves the use of a personal computer and software for writing, graphics, and page layout. Using DTP, documents can be created and edited, page layout and typography can be specified, and copy can be checked and approved. The manuscript can then be turned over to a service group to produce final laser-printed copy.

With desktop publishing, PCs can be turned into profit centers. Camera-ready copy can be produced for pennies per page, versus many times that for traditional typesetting.

Another advantage of DTP is that by using a modem, text can be written and transmitted over the telephone to a typesetter — or information can be obtained from on-line databases. The DTP system — a combination of research tool, typesetter, and page-layout software — works equally well using a PC or a Macintosh.

Putting together a cost-effective DTP system that will suit your particular needs can take time. To begin with, the hardware possibilities are tremendous — and growing rapidly with each passing month. (Even staying with one manufacturer — IBM, for example — you can be faced with hundreds of decisions.) As for software, there are dozens and dozens of word processors and thousands of graphics programs from which to choose.

Most PCs (IBMs and compatibles) use character-based software programs that run under MS-DOS as their operating system. This software displays only text on the screen. What you see on the screen, though, rarely looks at all like the finished output.

MS-DOS is a trademark of Microsoft Corporation. An acronym for Microsoft's Disc Operating system, it's called a disk operating system because a large part of its operation involves disks and disk files. Ever since IBM began installing Microsoft's disk operating systems in early versions of its PCs, MS-DOS has been one of the accepted standards for microcomputer operating systems.

In a sense, DOS can be considered the computer's traffic control center that keeps everything running smoothly. Recognized by the C> prompt that appears on your screen when DOS is ready to act on a command, MS-DOS is probably the most important program on your computer. It enables you to manage both hardware and software. In brief, DOS allows the computer to receive instructions, work with application programs, manage data files, and control information to the screen and other devices.

The original DOS, incidentally, was written by IBM for its Series-700 computers. It was one of the first major operating systems offered by a mainframe manufacturer.

The Macintosh operating system (which is built into every Macintosh), on the other hand, is based on a graphical user interface (GUI), which displays on the screen graphical icons that the user selects to operate the program. With this operating system, what you see on the screen usually corresponds closely to the printed page (what you see is what you get: WYSIWYG).

❑ ❑ ❑

"It's true that using WYSIWYG word-processing programs and laser printers results in very professional-looking newsletters," says Richard Huleatt, president and publisher of Information Intelligence Inc., (Phoenix, AZ) which publishes "Online Newsletter" and "Online Libraries and Microcomputers." "The additional effort required to 'fit' all articles into each page is still currently very time-consuming. Since we provide an up-to-date news service, we can't afford this time lag.

"If time permits, the use of WYSIWYG displays and laser printers may be appropriate. [But] if the news is late because it took longer to prepare [the newsletter], then you have no subscribers — and no newsletter."

❑ ❑ ❑

There are many more software titles for PCs than for Macintosh computers. Macintosh programs are generally superior, but PCs can be better for specialized business applications. Although the gap has narrowed, price remains one of the most compelling reasons to choose a PC clone over a Mac.

Two types of printers are used for desktop publishing: PostScript and non-PostScript. PostScript printers cost more, but they represent the professional standard for graphics and typesetting. They offer advantages in manipulation of text and graphics, compatibility with high-resolution output devices, and scalable fonts.

10.1 Word-Processing Applications

Virtually all word processors are used to process one very important product: information.

There are two principal methods of producing a newsletter: photocopying the output from a laser printer, and photo-offset. Provided a high-quality photocopying machine is used, the output from a laser printer can give a very satisfactory newsletter. Photocopying is best for newsletter quantities below a few hundred. Photo-offset, however, produces better quality and is the least expensive method for long runs.

10.2 DTP Applications

Newsletter publishing is probably the area of publishing for which DTP is best suited:

1) Newsletters are usually 8 1/2 by 11 inches in size — the size of publication that IBM PCs and Macintosh computers are best at creating.

2) Newsletters generally have small staffs — often only one or two people — and they can readily change their methods to make the most effective use of DTP.

3) Even one person using DTP can easily perform all the tasks involved — from editing and type creation to page layout and typesetting.

4) Typeset materials are more pleasing to read than typewritten copy, and typeset copy takes up less space than typescript does. Thus, DTP provides more information per page and lower printing and mailing costs. The result: higher quality at lower cost.

5) DTP allows typography to be used creatively, adding impact to the printed page.

6) Some newsletters can even be produced by using a partial DTP system.

❑ ❑ ❑

Overall, DTP can be used for many tasks: gathering information electronically, editing that information, writing new material, cutting and pasting, merging text with graphics, and creating graphics from numerical data. In addition, DTP can be used for gathering input from databases, handling mailing lists, tracking orders, preparing accounting and financial information, projecting costs, and managing time.

DTP can be useful regardless of the size of the task it's asked to handle. Not only are small publishers using DTP to turn out their newsletters, but large publishers have found it advantageous too. At the Library of Michigan (Lansing, MI), for example, almost 900 publications are produced electronically — including five regularly scheduled newsletters and others issued sporadically. A computer network makes it possible to produce material for publications on any of about 50 Macintosh computers and 15 laser printers.

❑ ❑ ❑

DTP is also widely used at the Association for Computing Machinery, Inc., a large publisher of multiple newsletters located in New York, New York. "Many of our newsletters are produced using desktop publishing," says Julie Eitzer, who handles the mechanics of publishing the various ACM newsletters. Eitzer receives camera-ready copy from the editors and coordinates printing in ACM's publications department.

Another example is Warren Publishing Inc., a large organization headquartered in Washington, D.C. This publisher routinely uses DTP in publishing nine of its twelve newsletters. (See TABLE 10-1.)

TABLE 10-1. At Warren Publishing Inc., nine of its 12 newsletters are produced using DTP.

Newsletter	Is DTP Used to Publish the Newsletter?
Audio Week	Yes
Common Carrier Week	Yes
Communications Daily	Yes
Early Warning Report	No
Facility Strategies	Yes
Mobile Satellite Reports	Yes
Public Broadcasting Report	Yes
Satellite Week	Yes
Space Commerce Week	Yes
Television Digest	No
TV + Cable Action Update	No
Video Week	Yes

❑ ❑ ❑

Probably the biggest advantage of desktop publishing is that it enables newsletters and other documents to be published more quickly. Take the Bowker Magazine Group of Cahner's Publishing Company, for example. The Bowker Group issues a wide range of publications including library-related journals and newsletters. Located in New York City, the Bowker Group publishes three journals (*Library Journal, School Library Journal,* and *Publishers Weekly*). The Group also publishes two newsletters ("Library Hotline" and "Corporate Library Update").

Historically — that is, before 1971, when its first newsletter was introduced — the Bowker Group published only the journals. In 1971, however, Karl Nyren, then senior editor of *Library Journal,* proposed that a "quick" newsletter be published on a weekly basis, in addition to the glossy journals. Such a newsletter would offer two main advantages. First, the newsletter would be highly selective and more immediate than any of the journals. In general, the newsletter would publish the following types of information:

- News having a deadline, such as grants and requests for proposals (RFPs): If, for example, the date of an upcoming meeting was changed at the last minute, the proposed newsletter could get the word out to people more promptly.
- News having a sense of immediacy, such as warnings and alerts: If, for instance, a product was malfunctioning, the newsletter could quickly notify readers of the problem.

The second advantage of publishing a newsletter was that job-bank information could be communicated more rapidly. Previously, when an employer advertised a job opening, it took so long sometimes for news of the opening to reach readers that the job had been filled by the time readers inquired. A newsletter, it was proposed, would turn around job information much more quickly, to the benefit of both employers and prospective employees.

The newsletter proposed by Nyren would be an early warning system for communicating with decision-makers. The journals, on the other hand, would continue to serve as working tools for the whole profession. That is, the journals would provide information of value to administrators, catalogers, collection development people, and others.

So, in 1971 — at the urging of Nyren — the Bowker Group launched its first newsletter. Initially called "LJ/SLJ Hotline," the name was changed to "Library Hotline" in 1985. (Refer to FIGURE 10-1 for a history of selected Bowker Group publications.)

In terms of function, "Library Hotline" focuses on information that has a sense of urgency, whereas the journals, since they have more space, are able to publish more detailed information.

"Before the days of 'Library Hotline,' says Susan DiMattia, its editor, "it often took as much as six weeks from the time copy was received from the authors, until printed journals reached our readers. Now the situation is different. Using my PC system with XYwrite software, I'm able to complete copy for each issue by noon on Wednesday. The copy then goes via modem to an Atex Editorial System (the same editorial system used in many newsrooms) in New York City,

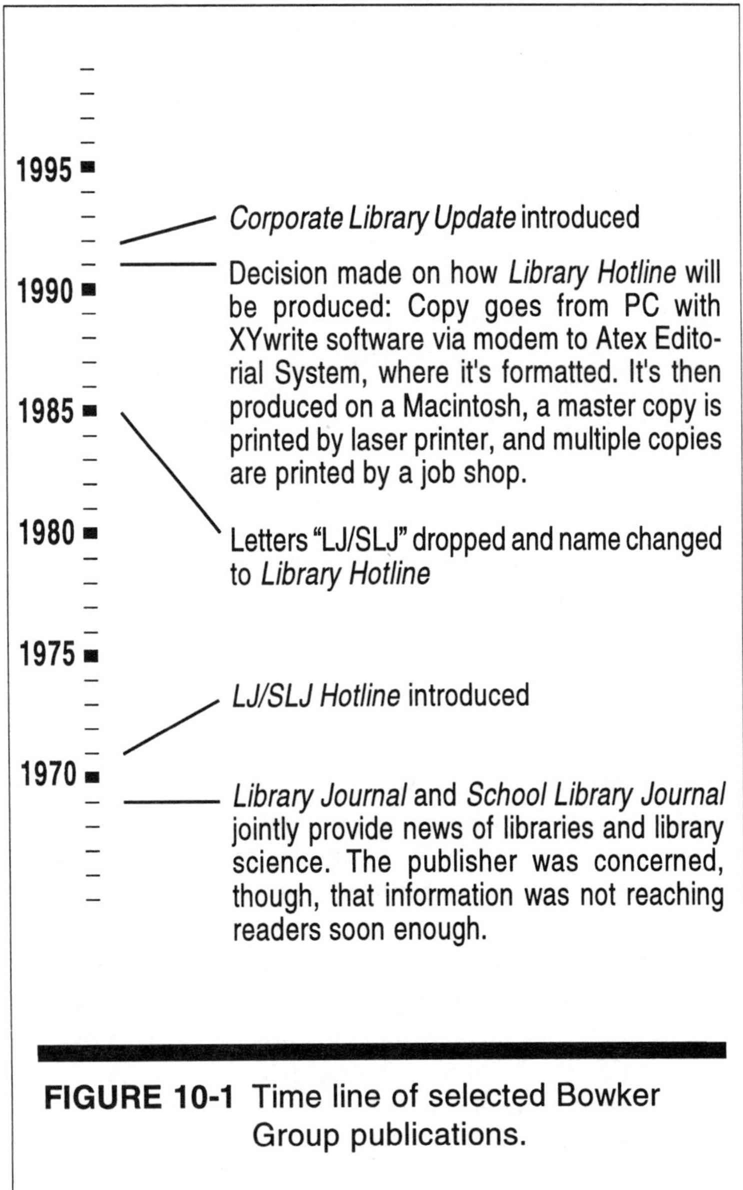

FIGURE 10-1 Time line of selected Bowker Group publications.

where it's formatted. From there, it's produced on a Macintosh. A master copy is then printed by laser printer and supplied to a job shop, where multiple copies are printed.

"The outcome? 'Library Hotline' now generally reaches its readers by the following Monday morning — less than six days after submission of copy."

In early 1992, a second newsletter, "Corporate Library Update," was launched by the Bowker Group. Although somewhat similar to "Library Hotline," this second newsletter is broader in scope. In addition to late-breaking news and new product announcements, for example, "Corporate Library Update" presents tips on managing information — tips that aren't usually published in "Library Hotline."

"Occasionally," says DiMattia, "'Corporate Library Update' will publish what we call an 'opinion piece' (it's almost an editorial) on some topic of current concern."

❑ ❑ ❑

While most newsletter editors using DTP consider commercial DTP equipment entirely satisfactory for publishing newsletters, some, such as Richard Huleatt, editor of "Online Newsletter," think differently: "We don't use DTP on our newsletters because we're waiting for a laser printer capable of printing at 600 dots-per-inch (dpi) or higher, instead of the present 300 dpi."

❑ ❑ ❑

Atex, Inc., an Eastman Kodak Company subsidiary located in Billerica, MA, has long been at the top among vendors of publishing systems for newspapers and magazines. Lately, Atex shifted to a modular product approach and began supplying modules for DTP.

For the most part, Atex's market has been newspapers, magazines, and highly designed catalogs; the company has not been a supplier of DTP systems to newsletter publishers. Nevertheless, Atex systems have been routinely used to produce the company's internal newsletters, as well as several customer newsletters.

"The products we sell can certainly be used to produce newsletters," says Don Hollands, vice president and general manager in Atex's General Publishing Products Division.

❑ ❑ ❑

As the total number of DTP systems in use increases, the number of newsletters that tell readers how to select and use DTP equipment also increases. Take the "Printing Association of Florida Newsletter," a membership publication of the Printing Association of Florida, Inc. According to Gene M. Strul, editor of this newsletter, many of its members are involved with DTP. "Naturally," says Strul, "our members are interested in reading about such products as laser printers; that's why information on DTP developments is included in our newsletter. We're now publishing 'Printing Association of Florida Newsletter' by DTP, using Macintosh and Aldus PageMaker software."

❑ ❑ ❑

There are over 40 million personal computers in place in the United States, according to Peter H. Lewis of the *New York Times*. Increasing numbers of these are being used for desktop publishing. In general, newsletters need powerful DTP, formatting, and graphical tools. And new items of hardware and software for DTP are being introduced into the marketplace almost daily. Take TrueType, for example, a new type technology from Apple Computer, Inc., and the Microsoft Corporation. According to Microsoft, TrueType will have all the advantages of software font scaling, with none of the problems. Microsoft also claims that TrueType will be faster than other font scalers and will avoid compatibility problems.

TrueType improves the way text appears on the computer screen and in printed documents. It permits the user to make the type as small or as large as desired, and it eliminates jagged lines and broken curves. According to Microsoft, TrueType will open up the world of scaled fonts to a whole new group of users.

❑ ❑ ❑

Now that the DTP technology is capable of producing much more sophisticated publications than previously, it is being referred to increasingly as "electronic publishing." And if the state of the art of DTP continues to make advances, it may not be long before it will be known simply as "publishing." One sign of the changing technology: Over the past decade, chief information officers (CIOs) — the executives who manage corporate computer systems — have come into the upper ranks of many companies. Here, they are (or soon will be) in a position to make even further advances in the DTP technology. When Chase Manhattan Bank, for instance, named a senior vice president, Craig Goldman, to the newly created position of CIO for all parts of the bank, *The New York Times* reported the following on December 20, 1991: "The aim ... is to increase the capabilities of desktop computers, and to make a global network that is available to all parts of Chase. The computer is not going to replace a smart lending officer, but the computer can provide information that lets them make decisions faster."

10.3 Examples of Personal Computers, Software, and Laser Printers for Word Processing And/or DTP

Selecting components for word processing and/or DTP can take up a great deal of a first-time buyer's time. In fact, personal computer, software and laser printer technologies have been changing so rapidly that even experienced users sometimes don't have time to make the best selection.

The following sections present examples of hardware and software often used to produce newsletters. The information given here is not intended as a shopping guide, but is, rather, a random selection of a few of today's offerings for word processing, DTP, and printing.

Three points should be kept in mind in looking at these examples:

1) Since the prices of hardware and software are continually changing, pricing information is not included here. (Prices have been declining steadily ever since the computer industry's inception.)

2) Only abbreviated specifications and performance highlights are presented here. (Complete information

on equipment and software can best be obtained from suppliers.)

3) For DTP, you should have at least a 20MB hard drive ... preferably 40MB or more.

10.3.1 Examples of Personal Computers for Word Processing and/or DTP

1) Apple Desktop Publishing System (Apple Computer, Inc., 20525 Mariani Avenue, Cupertino, CA 95014.)

A wide range of configurations of this system are available. A typical Apple system for DTP consists of a Macintosh Plus computer, a LaserWriter Plus printer, and selected software such as Microsoft Word 3.0. A whole new library of advanced applications software is available from Apple to answer virtually every desktop publishing need — including newsletters (from simple to elegant), graphs, and charts. The Apple DTP system features the following:

- The system handles layout tasks — such as resizing illustrations and adjusting kerning and leading — right on the screen.
- It drives any PostScript printer and commercial typesetting systems such as the Linotype Linotronic.

2) Apple Macintosh IIsi (Apple Computer, Inc., 20525 Mariani Avenue, Cupertino, CA 95014.)

Although all Macintosh PCs can be used for DTP, the IIsi is particularly well suited for this application. The Macintosh IIsi features the following:

- The IIsi is for people who need a powerful but affordable Macintosh system.
- The 68030 CPU lets you run Macintosh applica-

tions up to five times faster than the Macintosh Classic.

- Sound input lets you input your voice into newsletters.
- 1 megabyte of on-board RAM (expandable to 17 megabytes) lets you work with large amounts of data, such as scanned images.
- 512K of ROM enables color systems to display up to 16 million colors.
- The IIsi supports up to seven peripherals (such as CD-ROM).
- The MultiFinder operating system lets you cut and paste with ease.

10.3.2 Examples of Word Processors

Examples of word processors, or software, are described in the following paragraphs. Several points should be noted in regard to these examples:

- Windows word processors are an increasingly popular category of software. They provide a very useful environment for designing multi-column layouts and creating complex newsletters.
- Software selection involves hundreds of choices. At times, the final selection of software can wind up costing as much as the computer itself.
- Windows word processors require a 386-based system, 8MB to 15MB of hard disk space, and a VGA (or super-VGA) monitor.
- If you don't need the formatting and graphics capabilities of a Windows word processor, of course, you can save money by using a character-based word processor, such as WordPerfect 5.1.

1) Ami Pro 2.0* (Lotus Development Corp., Word

Processing Division, 1000 Abernathy Road, Building 400, Suite 1700, Atlanta, GA 30342.)

The editing, style-selection, and formatting capabilities of this Windows word processor make it very useful for newsletter work, especially where graphics are involved. Ami Pro 2.0 capabilities include the following:

- Powerful editing features; editing is quick and easy
- An excellent style sheet system
- Pop-up notes make editorial comments easy to use
- Powerful BASIC-like language
- Capable outliner and group-editing tools
- Provision for incorporating scanned images.

*Ami Pro is a trademark of Lotus Development Corporation.© Lotus Development Ccorporation. Used with permission.

2) WordPerfect 5.1 for Windows (WordPerfect Corporation, 1555 N. Technology Way, Orem, UT 84057)

Over the years, WordPerfect has been the most widely used of all word-processing programs. WordPerfect 5.1 for Windows provides the following features:

- With on-screen WYSIWYG fonts and graphics, you can manipulate and edit newsletters, correspondence, and technical reports quickly, with fewer mistakes.
- Quick List helps you search through directories and sub-directories in order to get to frequently needed files.
- The Button Bar lets you attach menu items or

macros to on-screen buttons and activate them with a click of the mouse.

- The Ruler makes formatting easy; it gives you access to features that take the work out of word processing.
- Both the mouse user and the keyboard user have the ability to easily integrate text and graphics.
- The Figure Editor makes it easy to add graphics.
- An Undo feature enables the user to quickly undo recently executed action.

3) Microsoft Word 5.5 (Microsoft Corp., One Microsoft Way, Redmond, WA 98052-6399)

Microsoft Word features fast performance;it's equipped with a Windows-like interface. Other features of Microsoft Word 5.5 include the following:

- Drop-down menus
- Versatility; for example, it permits bold and italics to be viewed on the screen.
- Dialog boxes and graphical page previews
- An outstanding outliner that permits the user to switch instantly between outline and full document.

4) Aldus© PageMaker© (Aldus Corporation, 411 First Avenue South, Seattle, WA 98104-2871.)

PageMaker version 4.0 features desktop publishing programs for the Apple Macintosh and the DOS-Windows 3.1 operating system. PageMaker allows you to "write, design, and produce professional-quality printed communications quickly and easily." Especially well suited for newsletters, PageMaker 4.0 features the following:

- When used with a laser printer, PageMaker produces output that is near-typeset quality. When used with an imagesetter, output is true typeset quality.

- Story Editor: Permits fast text entry and editing without exiting.
- Ability to condense or expand type from 5 to 250 percent.
- User-defined widow/orphan line control.
- Ability to generate tables of contents and indexes.

5) Microsoft Word for Windows 2.0 (Microsoft Corporation, One Microsoft Way, Redmond, WA 98052-6399.)

Microsoft Word for Windows 2.0 (also known as Word 2.0) provides the following:

- Unique Toolbar that lets you do those things you do most often — with one simple click of a button.
- Built-in drawing, charting, and shading features.
- Versatility: Existing WordPerfect files, as well as popular word-precessing file formats, are perfectly usable in Word 2.0.

10.3.3 Examples of Laser Printers for Word Processing and/or DTP

Today's laser printers are more sophisticated and faster than ever, and printed pages are sharper and more crisp. The laser printers described here have resolutions of 300 dots-per-inch; hence, print quality is high.

The performance of a printer depends on its intended application. For example: Will the printer be used for basic word processing? Or will it be used for more complex desktop publishing? A particular personal printer may give excellent performance on PageMaker for Windows 4.0, say, but perform poorly on a different word processor. In general, if you print out newsletters containing a lot of graphics, or if you download many fonts, you'll want at least 4MB of RAM so that you can get these jobs done quickly.

To improve the quality of text and graphics of your laser printer, enhancement boards can be plugged into the computer. (Most enhancement boards can be used with any printer built around a Canon laser engine.)

Two laser printers are briefly described in the following examples:

1) Epson ActionLaser II (Epson America, 20770 Madrona Ave., Torrance, CA 90503)

The Epson ActionLaser II is quick on the uptake, provides high-quality output, and is targeted specifically at first-time laser printer buyers: current dot matrix printer owners who want to upgrade to laser printing, first-time computer buyers, and people using laser printers at work who now want one at home. Other features of the ActionLaser II include the following:

- 14 resident fonts and HP-compatible font cartridge slot. (Accepts HP and third party industry standard font cartridges.)
- Fonts: Courier 10 & 12 pt. landscape and portrait Bold, Italic, and Regular
- EDP: 8.5 pt. landscape and portrait.
- 512 KB memory, expandable to 5.5 MB
- Cartridge slot: 1 HP compatible
- Features MicroArt printing and straight-through paper path
- Applications include DTP, business graphics,

word processing, spreadsheets, and envelope printing

2) Texas Instruments microLaser Plus PS17 (Texas Instruments, P.O. Box 6102, Airport Road, Temple, TX 76503-6102)

The microLaser Plus PS17 offers high speed and sturdy design. Other features of the microLaser Plus PS17 include the following:

- 17 font PostScript (The PS35 offers 35 fonts)
- High rated duty cycle: 10,000 pages per month
- Cartridge slots: 2
- Size: 190 sq. in. footprint
- PostScript: option

CHAPTER ELEVEN

Promote Your Newsletter

Survival of the Fittest

If your newsletter venture is being undertaken for profit, one of your principal concerns will be obtaining a sufficient number of paying subscribers. But even if your venture is being undertaken for other reasons, you will still want to have as many readers as possible.

Newsletter publishers have long sought a reliable formula for predicting circulation. For example, the following rule of thumb was suggested in 1982 by Howard Penn Hudson in the book *Publishing Newsletters* (Charles Scribner's Sons), in a section dealing with market penetration: "With business newsletters," wrote Hudson, "you should get 5 percent of your market for subscribers within the first two or three years."

To increase circulation, two main routes are open to you: advertising and direct marketing. Advertising consists mainly of advertising in print media, such as newspapers, magazines, and, in some cases, other newsletters. Direct marketing, the other main route for increasing circulation, includes direct mail, tip-ins, and telemarketing. For telemarketing, you will need names, phone numbers, and information about your audience. Other newsletters can provide you with assistance.

❑ ❑ ❑

As for direct mail, one approach is to rent a mailing list and prepare mailings soliciting additional subscribers. As an alternative, your local chamber of commerce may have a list of names you can use.

❑ ❑ ❑

Some newsletters use tip-ins asking readers to subscribe to their publications. Typically, in such instances, a card is inserted between pages of the stapled newsletter. The front of the card consists of a subscription form; the back contains the reply address of the publisher. One newsletter using such a tip-in in its November 1990 issue was ISI Institute for Scientific Information's newsletter "Science Watch."

11.1 Send Out Sample Newsletters

A particularly effective way to gain subscribers is to make an introductory offer of one or two issues of your newsletter, offering issues free of charge or for less than regular subscription price.

CHAPTER TWELVE

Reply Cards and Order Forms

It's All in the Cards

Reply cards and order forms serve many purposes when publishing a newsletter. Whether a particular card is called a reply card or an order form, depends, logically enough, on whether it's mainly used for replying or for ordering.

Reply cards are frequently used to sell literature — particularly in organization newsletters and outside corporate newsletters. For example, the organization newsletter "Library Hi Tech News," a monthly publication from Pierian Press (Ann Arbor, MI), often invites readers to order one or more items of Pierian Press literature. Items include special studies (published irregularly), back issues of the newsletter, and a bibliography — all ordered via forms printed in the newsletter.

12.1 Separate or Integral?

Experience has shown that more reply cards are

filled out and returned by readers when the cards are separate entities, rather than part of the newsletter.

12.2 Identify Hot Prospects by including Questions on Reply Cards

Reply cards can be used to gather useful information. Incoming reply cards haven't done their job, though, until they've been acted on fully. It will pay you to implement some type of system that will ensure that appropriate action has been taken on all incoming cards. One way to accomplish this is to print appropriate code letters on the cards. For example, code letters at the bottom of the card might indicate the following action:

M - Place on mailing list
MM - Attention: marketing manager
SR - Notify sales representative
L - Literature sent
A - Specific action:______________
F - All action taken; file reply card.

The person handling incoming reply cards circles the appropriate code letters on each card and writes in the initials of anyone who must take special action. Reply cards are then circulated throughout the organization for action or information. Only when all circled letters on the cards have been initialed is a card filed away. Experience has shown that without some such system, incoming cards may be mixed up by eager personnel when the cards first come in. As a result, some cards may be misplaced and never acted upon.

As indicated in FIGURE 12-1, you can also include statements on the reply card such as the following:

"Yes, I intend to purchase within 3/6/12 months," with instructions to circle as appropriate.

- Editor's Note: To be able to mail business reply cards for the standard postcard rate (19 cents), postal regulations require that cards be at least 3 1/2 by 5 inches in size, but not larger than 4 1/4 by 6 inches. Since there are also limits on card thickness, weight, and type layout, it's recommended that you show your local post office a sample of the card you propose using. (The post office can also provide information applying to cards that can be read automatically.)

FIGURE 12-1 Typical reply card

☐ Please send me information on ☐ X ☐ Y Other:__________
☐ Place my name on mailing list
☐ Send pricing information on:____________________
☐ for planned purchase ☐ for budgetary purposes
☐ I intend to purchase within 3 / 6 / 12 months (circle one)
☐ Have representative call me for an appointment:

NAME ( ) TELEPHONE

COMPANY/INSTITUTION

ADDRESS

CITY STATE ZIP

Comments/Suggestions:

M MM SR L A: F ☐☐

12.3 Ask for Comments and Suggestions

Leaving space on the card for comments and suggestions offers readers an opportunity to enter their opinions and make suggestions. Such information can be helpful when you are putting together future issues of your newsletter. Experience in writing and editing many newsletters has shown that readers are much more inclined to write in positive comments than negative ones.

12.4 Reply Card Response

In our experience, reply card response usually amounts to two to five percent of the mailing, but can run as high as 15 percent at times.

12.5 Code Reply Cards to Identify Issues of Newsletter

Include a small distinguishing mark, such as one or more boxes, in one corner of each reply card sent out on a particular mailing. An effective way to keep track of responses to mailings and cost-per-response is to use an electronic spreadsheet program, which is available for many personal computers.

12.6 Order Forms

Order forms are sometimes inserted in newsletters in place of reply cards. The November/December 1990 issue of "The Portable Paper," for example, was sent out with order forms and postage-paid reply envelopes stapled inside. These order forms enabled readers to order software or hardware products, subscriptions, or back issues of the newsletter. Information on how to order by phone/fax/mail, together with user testimonials of software and products, were also printed on the order forms used with "The Portable Paper."

CHAPTER THIRTEEN

Further Reading

From DTP to Typesetting

Printed material that deals in depth with writing or publishing newsletters is hard to find. Nevertheless, the resource material shown on the following pages may prove helpful. References are listed according to application: desktop publishing and word processing; newsletters; writing; typography and typesetting.

13.1 On Desktop Publishing and Word Processing:

Davis, Frederic E., John Barry, and Michael Wiesenberg, *Desktop Publishing*, Dow Jones-Irwin (Homewood, IL 60430), 1986, 310p

- Contains information for individuals and companies who are publishing, or planning to publish, a newsletter.

Dvirak, John C., *1992 Buyer's Guide to PCs, Printers, and Monitors*, Ziff-Davis Press (Emeryville, CA), 1991, 410p.

- Presents in-depth information on choosing the

computer system you need. Provides answers to such questions as:

- "What to look for in new and used desktop computers."
- "Which is best for you: a dot-matrix or laser printer?"

Hewson, David, *Introduction to Desktop Publishing*, Chronicle Books (San Francisco, CA), 1988, 112p.

- Discusses benefits of using DTP.

Johnson, Richard D., *Step-by-Step in Desktop Publishing*, Small Press, Vol. 8, No. 3, June 1990, 19-23.

Kleper, Michael L., *The Illustrated Handbook of Desktop Publishing and Typesetting*, Second Edition, Windcrest, TAB BOOKS, 1990, 927p.

Lanyi, Gabriel and Jon Barrett, *IBM Desktop Publishing*, Windcrest Books Division of TAB BOOKS INC. (Blue Ridge Summit, PA), 1989, 328p.

- Contains information on assembling a cost-effective DTP system. Evaluates PostScript vs. non-PostScript printers. Describes page-composition software, such as Ventura Publisher, PageMaker, Byline, GEM Desktop Publisher, and PagePerfect. Includes information on word processing software, such as WordStar, WordPerfect, and Word.

Lowe, Richard B. (Institute for Scientific Information, Philadelphia, PA) *Desktop Publishing and Resource Management*, Technical Communication, Vol 37, No. 2, May, 1990, 112-115.

Makuta, Daniel J. and William F. Lawrence, *Complete Desktop Publisher*, COMPUTE! Publications, Inc. (Part of ABC Consumer Magazines, Inc., Greensboro, NC), 1986, 293p.

- This comprehensive guide on personal publishing includes information on use of computer-generated graphics; selecting page-layout software; and dealing with typographers, printers, and designers.

Morganstern, S., *HELP! II*, Home Office Computing, 7:28+, N, 1989

• Reviews five sources of information on DTP

McIlroy, Thad, *The Evangelist of Desktop Publishing*, Small Press, Vol. 8, No. 3, June, 1990, 8-9

Rosenzweig, Sandra et al, *1991 Buyer's Guide*, Vol. 5, No. 10, Oct., 1990, 71-168.

13.2 On Newsletters:

Darnay, Brigitte, *The National Directory of Newsletters and Reporting Services*, Gale Research Co. (Book Tower, Detroit, MI 48226)

Dubrovin, Vivian, *Creative Word Processing*, A Language Power Book, 1987, 112p.

• Describes the different types of newsletters; lists organizations that might be interested in starting a newsletter, such as Scout groups, church youth groups, and civic organizations. Gives examples of single-and multiple-column newsletters.

Practical suggestions made by the author include the following:

- Even though an organization may not want a newsletter on a continuing basis, it may be interested in one or a few instructional newsletter issues for a specific event.
- Plan your newsletter before you start writing.
- Save all newsletter files on the same disk.

- Always tell newsletter readers how to obtain further information.
- Word processing makes the writing and printing process easy enough for anyone to produce a newsletter.

Goss, Frederick D., *Success in Newsletter Publishing, A Practical Guide*, 3rd Edition, The Newsletter Publishers Association (1401 Wilson Boulevard, Suite 207, Arlington, VA 22209), 1988, 272p.

- This hardback is a practical guide to starting, operating, and marketing a commercial newsletter.

Gregory, H., *How to Make Newsletters, Brochures & Other Good Stuff Without a Computer System*, Pinstripe Publishing (P.O. Box 711, Sedro Woolley, WA 98284), 1987, 159p.

- Handbook on promotion planning, writing, and pasteup for small business and more. Includes information on formats, consistency of mailings, use of photos, and preparation of mechanical.

Hudson, Howard P.,*The Newsletter on Newsletters*, The Newsletter Clearinghouse (44 West Market Street, Box 311, Rhinebeck, NY 12572)

- Provides information on "tracking the largely undocumented newsletter world, providing information and perhaps inspiration to newsletter entrepreneurs." Reports on the field, cites new titles, tracking trends, and news that can be difficult to find elsewhere.

Hudson, Howard P., *Newsletter Yearbook Directory*, The Newsletter Clearinghouse (44 West Market Street, Box 311, Rhinebeck, NY 12572).

- Available in soft-cover, this directory is a dual-purpose guide:

(1) The directory portion lists subscription news-

letters by subject, and indexed by geographic region, title, and multiple-newsletter publishers.

(2) The yearbook part of the directory includes historical information about newsletters and about the Newsletter Publishers Association. "It reviews the newsletter world of the preceding couple of years — events, conferences, awards, newsletters in the news."

Mitchell, Greg, *Cats, Chocolate, Clowns, and Other Amusing, Interesting and Useful Subjects Covered by Newsletters*, Dembner Books, Red Dembner Enterprises Corp., 1982, 189p.

- The introduction to this book states "Pick a subject, any subject, and chances are that somewhere in America someone is publishing a newsletter, journal, or bulletin about it." Here are just a few of these, as listed in the book:
- American Lock Collectors Association Newsletter, 14010 Cardwell, Livonia, MI 48154: a 6-page bimonthly for 300 collectors of locks, keys, handcuffs, leg irons, and related material.
- Evelyn Waugh Newsletter, English Department, Nassau Community College, Garden City, NY 11530: All about the brash and eccentric author of *The Loved One* and many other books. Eight pages, 3 times a year.
- The Hollywood Scriptletter, 1626 N. Wilcox Ave., Hollywood CA 90028: An 8-page monthly with tips from, and interviews with, pros, for aspiring film/TV/theater writers.

Business Guide on Newsletter Publishing, Entrepreneur Group, 2392 Morse Avenue, P.O. Box 19797, Irvine, CA 92713-9438 (800-421-2300; in CA:800-352-7449).

Oxbridge Directory of Newsletters, Ninth Edition, Oxbridge Communications, Inc., 150 Fifth Avenue, Suite 636, New York, NY 10011, 1990, 1045p.

- A comprehensive guide to U.S. and Canadian newsletters, this directory provides information on 21,000 newsletters — divided into 167 categories. For example, the category Food lists 162 newsletters, Education 668, Computers & Automation 549, and Environment & Ecology 364.
- In addition to information on individual newsletters, the directory contains information on multi-publishers, list rentals, advertising rates, printing companies, and more.

13.3 On Writing:

Foster, Edward Halsey, *Style Manuals,* Small Press, Vol. 8, No. 3, June, 1990, 14-15; 18

13.4 On Typography and Typesetting

Burklund, Susan, *Tips on Typography," Desktop Publishing, Vol. VIII, Issue 9, 50-52.*

APPENDIX

Terms and Names

Two sets of information are found in the Appendix: Appendix A consists of a glossary of words and terms mentioned in the book. Appendix B consists of a list of the various newsletters cited in the book, broken down by Chapter. The names of publishers, editors, and other personnel working on these newsletters are also included.

APPENDIX A

Glossary

The following terms, which appear in the book, are defined here as an aid to readers:

Ada: A programming language designed by the U.S. Department of Defense. It is required for all Department of Defense projects, but is not yet widely used.

Advertising ratio: Ratio of advertising pages to editorial pages

Case history: An article focusing on an individual's use of a particular product

CD-ROM: Compact disk-read only memory is an emerging information storage and retrieval technology.

Circulation: Average number of copies of a publication sold over a given period

Database: An organized collection of information

Desktop publishing (DTP): The writing and production of a publication, such as a newsletter, using a desktop computer

Disclaimer: A statement that an article is not intended as an endorsement

DOS: Disk operating system; coordinates operation of the computer system

Dot matrix: A printer technology that uses a print head to produce text and graphics by means of arrays of dots dpi: Dots per inch; a measure of resolution or sharpness of image.

Electronic mail (E-mail): A way of sending messages over computer terminals.

Electronic publishing: Desktop publishing

E-mail: Electronic mail; exchange of messages via on-line service.

Filler: Short piece of copy for filling out a column

Franchise newsletter: A preprepared newsletter; a company can purchase a supply of preprinted newsletters, imprint its own name, and distribute completed newsletters to its customers.

GUI: Graphical user interface

House organ: Internal newsletter

IBM PC clone/compatible: IBM PC clones are personal computers that are very close in appearance and performance to PCs in the IBM PC family. IBM PC compatibles, on the other hand, although very close to IBM PCs in functionality, may differ from them in appearance.

Interviewee: One who is interviewed, such as for a case history article

Macintosh: The Apple Macintosh family was first introduced in 1984 and is well known for its graphical user interface, networking capabilities, and other features. The Mac family makes up the main non-IBM PC compatible line of computers, and is well suited for desktop publishing and graphics.

Memory: Either read/write random access memory (RAM) or read only memory (ROM)

Microprocessor: Another name for processor, CPU, or chip.

Photo-offset: A method of printing based on photolithography, in which the inked image is transferred from a metal plate to a rubber surface — and from there to paper.

Random access memory (RAM): Computer memory used to store information and programs, perform calculations, and control computer operation.

Read only memory (ROM): Memory permanently encoded on a chip in the computer.

RS-232C: An electrical standard established by the Electrical Industries Association

Selective binding: A technology used by some publications to produce customized editions.

Self-mailer: A printed piece, such as a newsletter, that can be mailed without an envelope

Sign-off: Approval

Software: Programs, such as word processors, that tell the computer what tasks to perform.

Special-interest-group (SIG) newsletter: Contains information for readers having a common interest

Stylebook: A style manual, or reference, describing accepted standards of punctuation, abbreviations, etc.

"Tip-in": Material inserted loosely between the pages of a newsletter or other publication

VAR: Abbreviation for value-added relicensor

Video graphics array (VGA): The graphics standard for IBM PC compatible computers. VGAs have analog, rather than digital, signals.

Window: An area of a computer system screen; in some cases, two or more windows can be viewed simultaneously or sequentially.

Word processor: Computerized system consisting of a keyboard, video display, memory storage on disks or tapes, and a high-speed printer. There are many different word-processing programs. They range from simple text editors to complicated programs for handling most of the different types of documents. Among the most popular word processors are Microsoft Word 5.5, WordPerfect 5.1, Lotus Ami Professional 1.2, and Microsoft Word for Windows 1.1.

Writer's guidelines: Instructions to would-be authors

WYSIWYG: An acronym meaning "What You See Is What You Get"; WYSIWYG refers to a computer system's ability to display documents on the screen exactly as they are printed out by a printer.

APPENDIX B

Newsletters, Publishers, and Personnel

CHAPTER TWO

Frederick D. Goss (Exec. Dir.)
Newsletter Publishers Association
1401 Wilson Blvd., Suite 207
Arlington, VA 22209 2

Satellite Week
Paul Warren (Sr. Ed.)
Warren Publishing Inc.
2115 Ward Ct, NW
Washington, DC 20037 2, 9

The Kiplinger Washington Letter
Austin Kiplinger
The Kiplinger Washington Editors, Inc.
1729 H St. NW
Washington, DC 20006 2, 3

Control Industry Inside Report
Felix Tancula (Ed.)
Cahners Publishing
A Division of Reed Publishing USA
827 Fairlawn Ave.
Libertyville, IL 60048 2, 5

Computer Graphics (and other ACM Newsletters)
Steve Cunningham (SIGGRAPH dir. for pubs. and ed. of Computer Graphics)
Donna Baglio (Assoc. dir. of ACM SIG Services)
Computer Science Dept.
Calif. State U. at Stanislaus
801 W Monte Vista
Turlock, CA 95380

Julie Eitzer (Promotions & Pub. Coord.)
ACM SIG Services Dept.
Assoc. for Computing Machinery, Inc.
1515 Broadway
New York, NY 10036 — 2

The Latham Letter
Madeleine C. Pitts
The Latham Foundation
Latham Plaza
1826 Clement Ave.
Alameda, CA 94501 — 2

LAMALUG: The Apple COREspondent
John Rummel (PI officer)
Lansing Area Mac & Lisa Users Group
P.O. Box 27372
Lansing, MI 48909 — Various chapters

Privacy Times Newsletter
Evan Hendricks (Pub.)
The Privacy Council
Washington, DC — 2

Edna Hibel Society Newsletter
Edna Hibel Society
P.O. Box 9721
Coral Springs, FL 33075 — 2

The Newsletter
Lila Roseman (Ed.)
Arthritis Foundation
New Jersey Chapter
200 Middlesex Turnpike
Iselin, NJ 08830 — 2, 3

Communications Briefings
Frank Grazian (Exec. Ed.)
A business newsletter based in
Camden County, NJ — 2

Hudson City Trends
Hudson City Savings Bank
Marketing Dept.
West 80 Century Rd.
Paramus, NJ 07652 — 2

News Notes
Frank LaPerch (Pres.)
Scientific Instruments
200 Saw Mill River Rd.
Hawthorne, NY 10532 — 2, 5

HealthLetter
AARP Pharmacy Service
P.O. Box 883
Libertyville, IL 60048 — 2

Turftips
Green-a-Lawn
(No address for pub.) — 2

Construction Supervision & Safety Letter
Anne A. Clement (Pub. Rel.)
Bureau of Business Practice
Simon & Schuster
24 Rope Ferry Rd.
Waterford, CT 06386 — 2, 5

Library Hi Tech News
Ken Wachsberger (Man. Ed.)
The Pierian Press
P.O. Box 1808
Ann Arbor, MI 48106 2, 4, 12

Payroll Administration Guide Newsletter
Rosalyn Rosenberg (Man. Ed.)
The Bureau of National Affairs, Inc.
1231 25th St. NW
Washington, DC 20037 2

Alumni, the Newsletter for Notre Dame Alumni
Notre Dame Alumni Assoc.
201 Main Building
Notre Dame, IN 46556 2, 4

The Portable Paper
Hal Goldstein (Coed.)
Thaddeus Computing, Inc.
P.O. Box 869
Fairfield, IA 52556 2, 3, 5, 12

Apple Library Users Group Newsletter
Monica Ertel (Ed.)
Apple Computer, Inc.
10381 Bandley Drive (MS82)
Cupertino, CA 95014 2, 9

Market Newsletter
The Writer
120 Boyleston St.
Boston, MA 02116 2

Newsletter
Elderhostel Catalog
Federal St.
Boston, MA 02110 2

NCGA Forum replaced by two inserts:
NCGA News and NCGA CAD/CAM File
Andrew Barauskas (Mktg. Coord.)
James A. Schuping (Pres. and CEO)
National Computer Graphics Assoc. (NCGA)
2722 Merrilee Dr., Suite 200
Fairfax, VA 22031-4499 2

CHAPTER THREE

Food Protection Report
Charles Felix (Ed.)
Charles Felix Assoc.
P.O. Box 1581
Leesburg, VA 22075 3, 4

Brain & Strategy
Dudley Lynch (Ed.)
Brain Technologies Corp.
P.O. Box 507
Fort Collins, CO 80522 3

The Portable Paper
Hal Goldstein (Coed.)
Thaddeus Computing, Inc.
P.O. Box 869
Fairfield, IA 52556 3, 2, 5, 12

TIS NEWS
Aldo Conetta
Technicon Industrial Systems
Tarrytown, NY 10591 3, 4

The DOS Authority
Douglas Cobb (Pub.)
Tracy Smith
The Cobb Group, Inc.
9420 Dunsen Parkway, Suite 300
Louisville, KY 40220 3, 5

Network Consultant Quarterly
Ned Stirlen (Ed.)
Telematics International Inc.
1201 Cypress Creek Rd.
Fort Lauderdale, FL 33309 3, 5

Offline
David Dumkowski (Community Relations)
Tacoma Public Library
1102 Tacoma Ave. South
Tacoma, WA 3

ADA News
Judith Jakush (Ed.)
ADA Publishers, Inc.
211 E. Chicago Ave.
Chicago, IL 60637 3

Water News
Elizabeth B. Crumbley (Ed.)
Virginia Water Resources Research Center
Virginia Polytechnic Inst. and State U.
617 North Main Street
Blacksburg, VA 24060-3397 3

The Newsletter
Lila Roseman (Ed.)
Arthritis Foundation
New Jersey Chapter
200 Middlesex Turnpike
Iselin, NJ 08830 3, 2

Computer Communication Review
Craig Partridge (Past Ed., ACM SIGCOMM Computer Comm. Review)
Bolt Beranek & Newman
824 Kipling St.
Palo Alto, CA 94301-2831 3, 5

The Thermogram
The DuPont Company
Instrument Products Div.
Wilmington, DE 19898 3

Microprocessor Report 3

The Kiplinger Washington Letter
Austin Kiplinger
The Kiplinger Washington Editors, Inc.
1729 H St. NW
Washington, DC 20006 3, 2

CHAPTER FOUR

Printing Association of Florida Newsletter
Gene Strul (Ed.)
Printing Association of Florida, Inc. (PAF)
P.O. Box 170010
Hialeah, FL 33017-0010 4, 5, 7, 10

Food Protection Report
Charles Felix (Ed.)
Charles Felix Assoc.
P.O. Box 1581
Leesburg, VA 22075 4, 2, 3

Communication Resources 4

Moneysworth 4

mixin'
American Bartenders Assoc. 4, 3

The Migrant
Michigan Audubon Society 4, 3

New Waves
Texas Water Resources Inst.
Texas A&M Univ. 4, 3

.dbf 4

Ada Letters
ACM Press
Assoc. for Computing Machinery, Inc.
11 West 42nd St.
New York, NY 10036 4

Atex Times
Don Hollands (VP & Gen. Mgr. of Atex General Publishing Products Div.)
Bill Machovec (Ed.)
Michael Akillian
Atex Inc.
805 Middlesex Turnpike
Billerica, MA 01821-3914 4, 10

Perspective 4

Reference(Clipper)
Joyce Bentley
Charles Bestor (Sr. Ed.)
Pinnacle Publishing, Inc.
P.O. Box 1088
Kent, WA 98035-1088 4, 2, 5

The Quick Answer 4

Library Hi Tech News
Ken Wachsberger (Man. Ed.)
The Pierian Press
P.O. Box 1808
Ann Arbor, MI 48106 4, 2, 12

Alumni, the Newsletter for Notre Dame Alumni
Notre Dame Alumni Assoc.
201 Main Building
Notre Dame, IN 46556 4, 2

The NEWSLETTER
George O. Hewson (Sec.)
Retired United Pilots Ass'n. (RUPA)
218 Highland Ave.
Piedmont, CA 94611-3710 4

TIS NEWS
Aldo Conetta
Technicon Industrial Systems
Tarrytown, NY 10591 4

Online Newsletter
Richard S. Huleatt (Pres. and Pub.)
Information Intelligence Inc.
P.O. Box 31098
Phoenix, AZ 85046 4, 5, 10

Online libraries and Microcomputers
George Machovev (Ed.)
Information Intelligence Inc.
P.O. Box 31098
Phoenix, AZ 85046 4, 5, 10

Dun's Dataline
Pamela Shipp (D&B Info. Ser.)
Dun's Marketing Services
A company of the Dun & Bradstreet Corp.
3 Sylvan Way
Parsippany, NJ 07054-3896 4, 5

COSMEP newsletter
COSMEP, Inc.
The International Association of Independent Publishers
P.O. Box 703
San Francisco, CA 94101

The Business Week NewsLetter of Information Executives (discontinued)
McGraw-Hill, Inc. 4

The SenTInel (discontinued) 4

The TImes
Thor M. Firing (Ed.)
Santa Clara Valley TIPC Users Group
55 Temescal Terrace
San Francisco, CA 94118 4

CHAPTER FIVE

Reference(Clipper)
Joyce Bentley
Charles Bestor (Sr. Ed.)
Pinnacle Publishing, Inc.
P.O. Box 1088
Kent, WA 98035-1088 5, 2, 4

Various Newsletters
John Rummel (Pub. Info.)
Library of Michigan
P.O. Box 30007
717 West Allegan St.
Lansing, MI 48909 Various

Network Consultant Quarterly
Ned Stirlen (Ed.)
Telematics International Inc.
1201 Cypress Creek Rd.
Fort Lauderdale, FL 33309 5, 3

View from the Ledge
Chuck Shepherd (Ed.)
P.O. Box 57141
Washington, DC 20037 5

The Portable Paper
Hal Goldstein (Coed.)
Thaddeus Computing, Inc.
P.O. Box 869
Fairfield, IA 52556 5, 2, 3, 12

Dun's Dataline
Pamela Shipp (D&B Info. Ser.)
Dun's Marketing Services
A company of the Dun & Bradstreet Corp.
3 Sylvan Way
Parsippany, NJ 07054-3896 5, 4

News notes
Frank LaPerch (Pres.)
Scientific Instruments
200 Saw Mill River Rd.
Hawthorne, NY 10532 5, 2

Control Industry Inside Report
Felix Tancula (Ed.)
Control Engineering
Cahners Publishing
A Division of Reed Publishing USA
827 Fairlawn Ave.
Libertyville, IL 60048 5,2

Construction Supervision & Safety Letter
Anne A. Clement (Pub. Rel.)
Bureau of Business Practice
Simon & Schuster
24 Rope Ferry Rd.
Waterford, CT 06386 5, 2

New from Japan
Roy Roecker (Pub.)
Prestwick Publishing, Inc.
390 N. Federal Highway, Suite 401
Deerfield Beach, FL 33441 5

New from Europe
Roy Roecker (Pub.)
Prestwick Publishing, Inc.
390 N. Federal Highway, Suite 401
Deerfield Beach, FL 33441 5

New from U.S.
Roy Roecker (Pub.)
Prestwick Publishing, Inc.
390 N. Federal Highway, Suite 401
Deerfield Beach, FL 33441 5

Electronics from the World
Roy Roecker (Pub.)
Prestwick Publishing, Inc.
390 N. Federal Highway, Suite 401
Deerfield Beach, FL 33441 5

Printing Association of Florida Newsletter
Gene Strul (Ed.)
Printing Association of Florida, Inc. (PAF)
P.O. Box 170010
Hialeah, FL 33017-0010 5, 4, 7, 10

Science Watch
David A. Pendlebury (Ed.)
ISI Institute for Scientific Information
3501 Market St.
Philadelphia, Pa 19104 5, 11

SB News
Mary Ellen Seitz
Dr. George Poste (Ch. of R&D for SB)
SmithKline Beecham (SB)
1 Franklin Plaza
P.O. Box 7929
Phildelphia, PA 19101 5

Fillers for Publications
Pat Johnston (Mgr.)
Fillers for Publications
7015 Prospect Pl. NE
Albuquerque, NM 87110 5

The DOS Authority
Kathleen Lane
Melissa Halberlin
The Cobb Group, Inc.
9420 Bunsen Parkway, Suite 300
Louisville, KY 40220 5, 3

Inside Turbo C++
Kathleen Lane
Melissa Halberlin
The Cobb Group, Inc.
9420 Bunsen Parkway
Suite 300
Louisville, KY 40220 5, 3

Computer Communication Review
Craig Partridge (Past Ed., ACM SIGCOMM Computer Comm. Review)
Bolt Beranek & Newman
824 Kipling St.
Palo Alto, CA 94301-2831 5, 3

Online Newsletter
Richard S. Huleatt (Pres. and Pub.)
Information Intelligence Inc.
P.O. Box 31098
Phoenix, AZ 85046 5, 4, 10

Online libraries and Microcomputers
George Machovec (Ed.)
Information Intelligence Inc.
P.O. Box 31098
Phoenix, AZ 85046 5, 4, 10

CHAPTER SEVEN

Library Hotline
Susan DiMattia (Ed. Office)
44 Chatham Rd.
Stamford, CT 06903
(mailing address)

Bowker Magazine Group
The Cahners Publishing Co.
Div. of Reed Publishing USA
249 W 17th St.
New York, NY 10011 7, 10

Microwave News
Lois Slesin (Ed.) 7

Government WasteWatch
Mark Q. Rhoads (Ed.)
Citizens Against Government Waste
Suite 400
1301 Connecticut Ave., NW
Washington, DC 20036 7

The Weekly Report to the People
Gerry E. Stodds (U.S. Rep.)
Democrat, Massachusetts 7

OR ServiceLine
Linda Winikow (VP-Cor. Pol. and Ext. Af.)
James E. Lois (Mgr. Cor. Com.)
OR Orange and Rockland Utilities, Inc.
One Blue Hill Plaza
Pearl River, NY 10965 7

Printing Association of Florida Newsletter
Gene Strul (Ed.)
Printing Association of Florida, Inc. (PAF)
P.O. Box 170010
Hialeah, FL 33017-0010 7, 4, 5, 10

International Living
Kathleen Peddicord (Ed.)
824 E. Baltimore St.
Baltimore, MD 21202 7

Today's Parts Manager
(Ed.)
Management Computer systers
Columbus, OH 7

Sailaway
Matthew Wiseman (Man.Ed.)
Bill Bickler (Ed.)
Travel Agents Internt'l
Box 31005
St. Petersburg, FL 33731-8905 7

Nursing Mom
Jeanie Donaldson (Ed.)
Inyokern, CA 7

Securities Week
McGraw-Hill
(discontinued) 7

View
Anderson Ranch Arts Center
P.O. Box 5598
Snowmass Village, CO 81615 7

CHAPTER EIGHT

Cooper-Hewitt Newsletter
Smithsonian Associates
900 Jefferson Drive
Washington,DC 20560

Cooper-Hewitt National Museum of Design
Smithsonian Institution
2 E 91st Street
New York, NY 10128-6906 8

Phone Disc
Phone Disc USA Corp.
Marblehead, MA 8

Business Lists-on-Disc
American Business Infromation Inc.
Omaha, NB 8

CHAPTER NINE

Apple Library Users Group Newsletter
Monica Ertel (Ed.)
Apple Computer, Inc.
10381 Bandley Drive (MS82)
Cupertino, CA 95014 9, 2

Access
John Rummel (Pub. Info.)
Library of Michigan
P.O. Box 30007
717 West Allegan St.
Lansing, MI 48909 9, 2

Various Newsletters
Paul Warren (Sen. Ed.)
Warren Publishing Inc.
2115 Ward Ct., NW
Washington, DC 20037 Various

CHAPTER TEN

Online Newsletter
Richard S. Huleatt (Pres. and Pub.)
Information Intelligence Inc.
P.O. Box 31098
Phoenix, AZ 85046 10, 4, 5

Online libraries and Microcomputers
George Machovec (Ed.)
Information Intelligence Inc.
P.O. Box 31098
Phoenix, AZ 85046 10, 4, 5

Various Newsletters
John Rummel (Pub. Info.)
Library of Michigan
P.O. Box 30007
717 West Allegan St.
Lansing, MI 48909 Various

Various ACM Newsletters
Julie Eitzer (Promotions & Pub. Coord.)
ACM SIG Services Dept.
Assoc. for Computing Machinery, Inc.
1515 Broadway
New York, NY 10036 10, 5

Satellite Week and other newsletters
Paul Warren (Sr. Ed.)
Warren Publishing Inc.
2115 Ward Ct., NW
Washington, DC 62000 Various

Library Hotline
Susan DiMattia (Ed. Office)
44 Chatham Rd.
Stamford, CT 06903
(mailing address)

Bowker Magazine Group
The Cahners Publishing Co.
Div. of Reed Publishing USA
249 W 17th St.
New York, NY 10011 10, 7

Corporate Library Update
Susan DiMattia (Ed. Office)
44 Chatham Rd.
Stamford, CT 06903
(mailing address) 10

Bowker Magazine Group
The Cahners Publishing Co.
Div. of Reed Publishing USA
249 W 17th St.
New York, NY 10011 10, 7

Atex Times
Don Hollands (VP & Gen. Mgr. of Atex General Publishing Products Div.)
Bill Machovec (Ed.)
Michael Akillian
Atex Inc.
805 Middlesex Turnpike
Billerica, MA 01821-3914 10, 4

Printing Association of Florida Newsletter
Gene Strul (Ed.)
Printing Association of Florida, Inc. (PAF)
P.O. Box 170010
Hialeah, FL 33017-0010 10, 4, 5, 7

CHAPTER ELEVEN

Science Watch
David A. Pendlebury (Ed.)
ISI Institute for Scientific Information
3501 Market St.
Philadelphia, PA 19104 11, 5

CHAPTER TWELVE

Library Hi Tech News
Ken Wachsberger (Man. Ed.)
The Pierian Press
P.O. Box 1808
Ann Arbor, MI 48106 12, 2, 4

The Portable Paper
Hal Goldstein (Coed.)
Thaddeus Computing, Inc.
P.O. Box 869
Fairfield, IA 52556 12, 2, 3, 5

CHAPTER THIRTEEN

The Newsletter on Newsletters
Howard P. Hudson (Ed.)
The Newsletter Clearinghouse
44 West Market St., Box 311
Rhinebeck, NY 12572 13

Index